design basics inc.®

Gold Seal
HOME PLANS ™

Favorites

TO OUR VALUED CUSTOMERS

Since 1983, we at Design Basics have been bringing people home with many of America's most popular home plans. Our company began as a custom home plan design firm for the professional builders of our local community, Omaha, NE. As the popularity of our designs increased, we expanded our focus from designing for the local market only, to designing plans that would be adaptable anywhere. Since then, builder as well as consumer interest in our plans has grown tremendously in all 50 states and countries around the world.

Today, we are one of the nation's largest home plan design services, offering a variety of home plans as well as products and services which include: color renderings, estimator's material lists, plan changes and more.

Whether it's one of our home plans, a product or service, we take pride in serving you with our very best. It's all a part of our culminating efforts to lead people to their dreams of home.

Design Basics . . . *"Bringing People Home."*

HOME PLANS

Timeless quality and precise detail are combined to provide home plans designed with attention to today's buyer and practicality for today's builder.

SERVICE INFORMATION

Gold Seal™ Favorites
is published by
Design Basics Inc.
11112 John Galt Boulevard
Omaha, NE 68137-2384
Text and design copyright © 1997
by Design Basics Inc.

Cover Photo: Plan #LGS3246 - The 'Jennings,' as seen on page 81. **Builder:** Kuszmaul Builders

Library of Congress Number: 97-095342
ISBN: 0-9647658-9-6

· INDEX ·

COPYRIGHT
Cans & Cannots

These days, it seems almost everybody has a question about what can or cannot be done with copywritten home plans. At Design Basics, we know US copyright law can sometimes get complex and confusing, but here are a few of the basic points of the law you'll want to remember.

Once you've purchased a plan from us and have received a Design Basics construction license,

You Can . . .

■ Construct the plan as originally designed, or change it to meet your specific needs.

■ Build it as many times as you wish *without* additional re-use fees.

■ Make duplicate blueprint copies as needed for construction.

You Cannot . . .

■ Build our plans without a Design Basics construction license.

■ Copy *any* part of our original designs to create another design of your own.

■ Claim copyright on changes you make to our plans.

■ Give a plan to someone else for construction purposes.

■ Sell the plan.

PROTECT YOUR RIGHTS

to build, modify and reproduce our home plans with a Design Basics construction license.

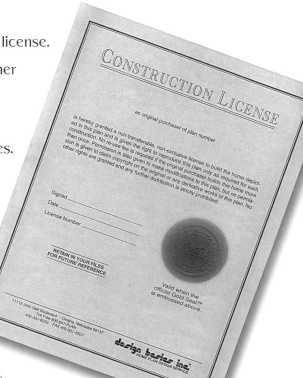

RANCH HOMES

LGS1129-11 Calumet

PRICE CODE

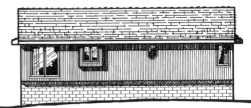

▶ High quality, erasable, reproducible vellums
▶ Shipped via 2nd day air within the continental U.S.

- convenient split-entry ranch design
- 2-car garage
- large entry with coat closet on entry level
- volume ceiling for visual expansion
- efficient kitchen with snack bar, lazy Susan and window over sink

- basement area accessed from entry and garage, allowing for a variety of finishing options
- hallway segregates all bedrooms from primary living areas for privacy

- double doors open to large master bedroom with vaulted ceiling
- walk-in closet and private 3/4 bath complete the master suite
- secondary bedrooms share convenient hall bath

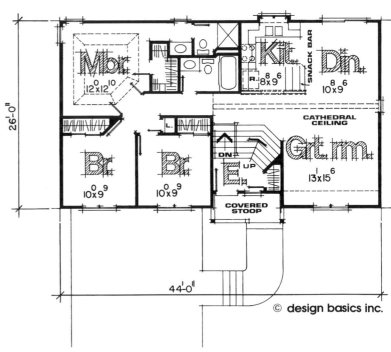

Rear Elevation

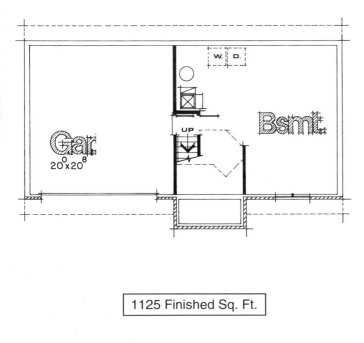

1125 Finished Sq. Ft.

© design basics inc.

ORDER DIRECT
7:00-6:00 Mon.-Fri. CST
800-947-PLAN

6

LGS3102-13 Aspen

PRICE CODE

▸ High quality, erasable, reproducible vellums
▸ Shipped via 2nd day air within the continental U.S.

- arched entry highlights brick and siding elevation
- great room with arched windows creates beautiful view from entry

- kitchen features large snack bar and convenient access to spacious utility room
- window at sink overloooks versatile covered area outside

- back door well located between family activity areas
- secondary bedrooms share hall bath
- master suite contains generous walk-in and whirlpool bath with compartmented stool and shower

Rear Elevation

Parade Home Package
available for all plans

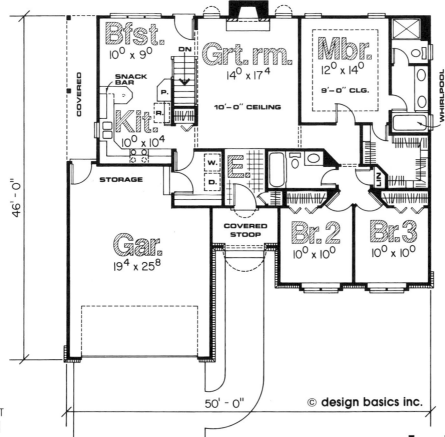

1339 Finished Sq. Ft.

ORDER DIRECT
7:00-6:00 Mon.-Fri. CST
800-947-PLAN

design basics inc. ®
HOME PLAN DESIGN SERVICE

LGS2761-13 Mayberry

PRICE CODE

▶ High quality, erasable, reproducible vellums
▶ Shipped via 2nd day air within the continental U.S.

Gold Seal HOME PLANS

- offering basement or alternate slab foundation, this home is the epitome of economy and efficiency
- practical design with no wasted space offers amenities typically offered only in larger plans

- sloped ceiling, and fireplace flanked by large windows expands the great room
- kitchen is exceptionally well planned featuring large pantry, 2 lazy Susans and snack bar serving the dinette

- strategically located TV cabinet/entertainment center with lazy Susan affords viewing from great room, dinette or kitchen
- master suite features large walk-in closet and deluxe bath area with dual lavs and glass panel separating shower and whirlpool

Rear Elevation

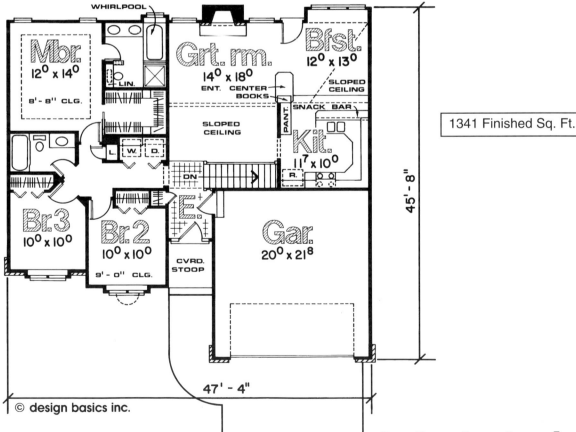

WHIRLPOOL

Mbr. 12⁰ x 14⁰
8'-8" CLG.

LIN.

Grt. rm. 14⁰ x 18⁰
ENT. CENTER BOOKS
SLOPED CEILING

Bfst. 12⁰ x 13⁰
SLOPED CEILING
SNACK BAR

PANT.

Kit. 11⁷ x 10⁰
R.

L. W. D.

DN

E.

Br.3 10⁰ x 10⁰

Br.2 10⁰ x 10⁰
9'-0" CLG.

CVRD. STOOP

Gar. 20⁰ x 21⁸

1341 Finished Sq. Ft.

45'-8"

47'-4"

© design basics inc.

ORDER DIRECT
7:00-6:00 Mon.-Fri. CST
800-947-PLAN

design basics inc.
HOME PLAN DESIGN SERVICE

LGS3010-PRICE CODE **14** Quimby

Gold Seal
HOME PLANS ™

▶ High quality, erasable, reproducible vellums
▶ Shipped via 2nd day air within the continental U.S.

- small ranch home makes grand statement with prominent entry
- 12-foot-tall ceiling integrates great room, semi-formal dining room and kitchen
- spacious covered porch accessed from dining room

- arched openings to kitchen with built-in bookcases provide dramatic backdrop for dining area
- efficient kitchen features 2 lazy Susans, plant shelf above upper cabinets and an airy window

- hall bath serves secondary bedrooms, with bedroom #3 easily optioned to a den
- master suite features a boxed 9-foot-high ceiling, whirlpool bath and walk-in closet
- space for work bench and sizeable storage area in garage

Rear Elevation

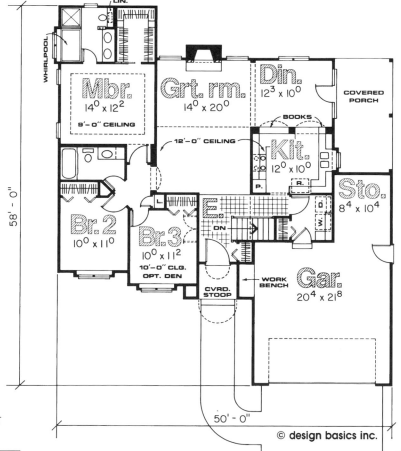

1422 Finished Sq. Ft.

© design basics inc.

9

design basics inc. ®
HOME PLAN DESIGN SERVICE

LGS1379-14 Pendleton

PRICE CODE

▶ **High quality, erasable, reproducible vellums**
▶ **Shipped via 2nd day air within the continental U.S.**

- optional elevation included with this plan at no additional cost
- formal dining room open to large entry with coat closet and wide stairs
- great room with vaulted ceiling and fireplace as focal point

- double L-shaped kitchen includes boxed window at sink, pantry, space saver microwave and buffet counter
- breakfast area with bayed window expands view
- convenient split-entry ranch design

- core hallway opens to large master bedroom with walk-in closet and private bath
- secondary bedrooms feature boxed windows and share centrally located hall bath

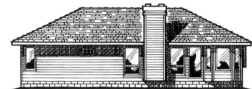

Rear Elevation

Alternate Elevation At No Extra Cost

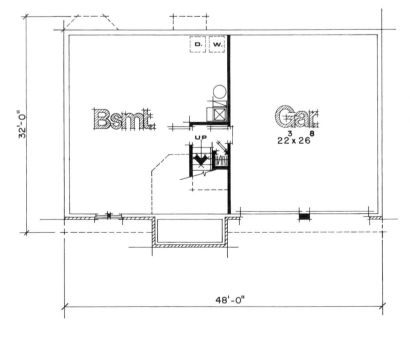

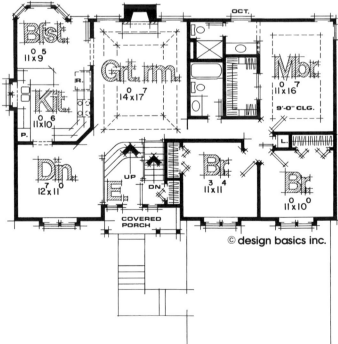

© design basics inc.

1429 Finished Sq. Ft.

ORDER DIRECT
7:00-6:00 Mon.-Fri. CST
800-947-PLAN

PRICE CODE
LGS3019-14 Kelsey

▶ **High quality, erasable, reproducible vellums**
▶ **Shipped via 2nd day air within the continental U.S.**

- covered porch adds charm to this ranch home
- sunny great room with 11-foot ceiling open to entry

- bowed breakfast area open to kitchen including island snack bar, corner sink and access to back yard
- secondary bedrooms share hall bath

- den with 10-foot-high ceiling and French doors options as a third bedroom
- volume master suite features whirlpool bath, dual lavs and mirrored doors to walk-in closet

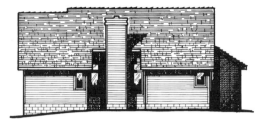

Rear Elevation

1479 Finished Sq. Ft.

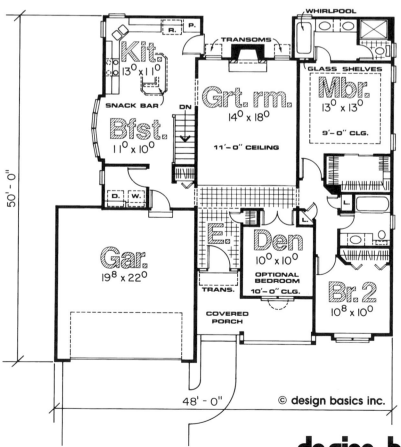

50' - 0"

Kit. 13⁰ x 11⁰

SNACK BAR

Bfst. 11⁰ x 10⁰

D. W.

TRANSOMS

DN

Grt. rm. 14⁰ x 18⁰

11'-0" CEILING

WHIRLPOOL

GLASS SHELVES

Mbr. 13⁰ x 13⁰

9'-0" CLG.

Gar. 19⁸ x 22⁰

E.

Den 10⁰ x 10⁰

OPTIONAL BEDROOM 10'-0" CLG.

TRANS.

COVERED PORCH

Br. 2 10⁸ x 10⁰

48' - 0"

© design basics inc.

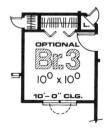

OPTIONAL
Br. 3 10⁰ x 10⁰
10'-0" CLG.

11

design basics inc.
HOME PLAN DESIGN SERVICE

▶ **High quality, erasable, reproducible vellums**
▶ **Shipped via 2nd day air within the continental U.S.**

Gold Seal ™
HOME PLANS

- pleasant mix of materials, shapes, and textures create notable elevation
- practical use of space is demonstrated by placement of 2 closets in entry
- optional den/bedroom provides design flexibility

- lofty great room features fireplace flanked by large windows
- double doors from great room offer privacy from kitchen
- dinette, featuring desk and snack bar also provides convenient access to outdoors

- garage features built-in workbench
- roomy laundry area is accessed from garage and kitchen
- master suite features deluxe bath with sloped ceiling and plant shelves above an open shower

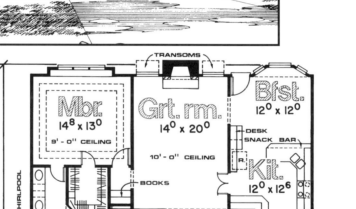

Rear Elevation

Parade
Home
Package
available for all plans

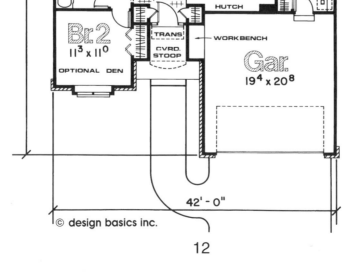

1499 Finished Sq. Ft.

ORDER DIRECT
7:00-6:00 Mon.-Fri. CST
800-947-PLAN

© design basics inc.

design basics inc.®
HOME PLAN DESIGN SERVICE

LGS679-15 Quincy

PRICE CODE

- dramatic high entry framed by columns and windows
- expansive great room features sloped ceilings to 11 feet and impressive fireplace surrounded by windows

- complete island kitchen includes lazy Susan, pantry and desk plus adjacent laundry area
- bright breakfast eating area
- formal ceiling in dining room

- vaulted ceiling in master bedroom with corner windows
- master bath features skylight and walk-in closet
- pleasant window sills in front bedrooms

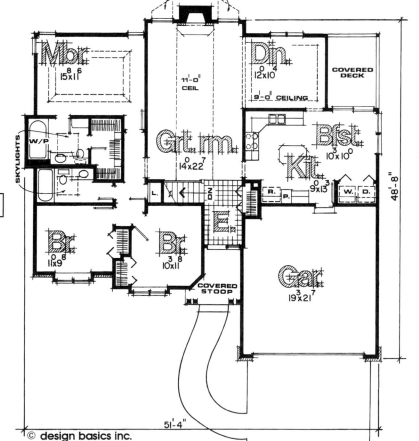

Rear Elevation

1511 Finished Sq. Ft.

TRAPS.

Mbr
15x11

11'-0"
CEIL

Dn
12x10

COVERED DECK

9'-0" CEILING

Grt. rm.
14x22

Bfst
10x10

Kit
9x13

SKYLIGHTS

W/P

Br
11x9

Br
10x11

Gar
19x21

COVERED STOOP

48'-8"

51'-4"

© design basics inc.

ORDER DIRECT

7:00-6:00 Mon.-Fri. CST

800-947-PLAN

design basics inc.®
HOME PLAN DESIGN SERVICE

LGS3555-15 Laramy

PRICE CODE

Gold Seal™
HOME PLANS

► High quality, erasable, reproducible vellums
► Shipped via 2nd day air within the continental U.S.

- windows and brick detailing perfect this warm elevation
- volume entry adorned with arched transom above door
- kitchen enjoys view to family room through arched opening above sink

- breakfast area has planning desk and boxed window
- covered porch off breakfast area welcomes relaxation
- cathedral ceiling adds drama to family room with fireplace framed by windows

- master bedroom has 9'-0" ceiling and view to back
- spacious walk-in closet, whirlpool under glass and dual sink vanity serve master bath
- bedroom #2 has volume ceiling and shares full bath with bedroom #3

Rear Elevation

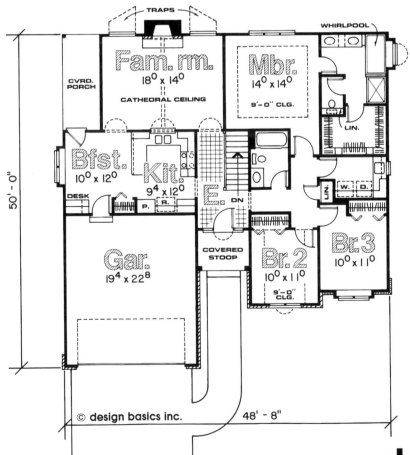

1518 Finished Sq. Ft.

© design basics inc.

48' - 8"

ORDER DIRECT
7:00-6:00 Mon.-Fri. CST
800-947-PLAN

design basics inc®
HOME PLAN DESIGN SERVICE

LGS3127-15 Haley

PRICE CODE

▸ High quality, erasable, reproducible vellums
▸ Shipped via 2nd day air within the continental U.S.

• corner wrapping porch provides focal point for cozy ranch
• entry open to great room with cathedral ceiling and formal dining room with 10-foot-high ceiling

• spacious kitchen features corner sink, built-in bookcase and shares snack bar with breakfast area
• bedroom wing has convenient laundry access

• plan offers versatility with optional third bedroom
• French doors open to master suite with volume ceiling, mirrored doors to walk-in closet and sunny whirlpool bath

Rear Elevation

Parade Home Package
available for all plans

1554 Finished Sq. Ft.

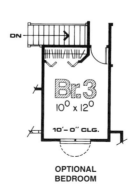

OPTIONAL BEDROOM

Bfst. 10⁰ x 11⁰
Grt. rm. 14⁰ x 20⁰
Br. 2 11² x 11⁰
Mbr. 13⁰ x 15⁰ 9'-0" CLG.
SNACK BAR
CATHEDRAL CEILING
Kit. 10⁰ x 13⁰
BOOKS
LIN.
52' - 8"
Br.3 10⁰ x 12⁰ 10'-0" CLG.
DN
CURIO
Din. 10⁰ x 14⁴ 10'-0" CLG.
OPTIONAL BEDROOM
COVERED PORCH
Gar. 19⁴ x 22⁰
WHIRLPOOL
50' - 0"
© design basics inc.

ORDER DIRECT
7:00-6:00 Mon.-Fri. CST
800-947-PLAN

15

HOME PLAN DESIGN SERVICE

LGS2537-15 Tahoe

PRICE CODE 15

- ▶ High quality, erasable, reproducible vellums
- ▶ Shipped via 2nd day air within the continental U.S.

- brick wing walls provide visually expansive front elevation
- from entry, traffic flows into bright great room with impressive 2-sided fireplace
- dining room opens to great room, offering view of fireplace

- French doors off entry open into kitchen
- kitchen features large pantry, planning desk and snack bar
- dinette accesses large, comfortable screen porch

- laundry room is strategically located off kitchen and provides for direct access from garage
- built-in shelves in garage
- French doors access master suite with formal ceiling and pampering bath

Rear Elevation

Parade Home Package
available for all plans

Den
$10^4 \times 13^4$
9'-0" CEILING

OPTIONAL DEN

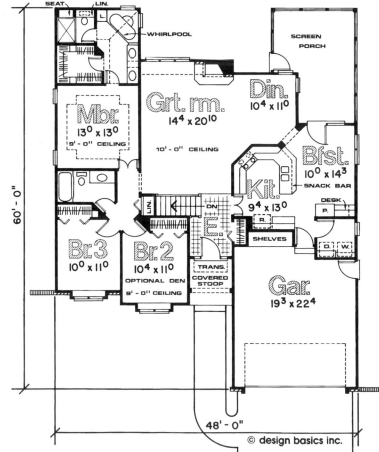

60'-0"

SEAT LIN.

WHIRLPOOL

Mbr.
$13^0 \times 13^0$
9'-0" CEILING

Grt. rm.
$14^4 \times 20^{10}$
10'-0" CEILING

SCREEN PORCH

Din.
$10^4 \times 11^0$

Bfst.
$10^0 \times 14^3$
SNACK BAR

Kit.
$9^4 \times 13^0$

DESK
P.

LIN.
DN

SHELVES

R.

D. W.

Br.3
$10^0 \times 11^0$

Br.2
$10^4 \times 11^0$
OPTIONAL DEN
9'-0" CEILING

TRANS.
COVERED STOOP

Gar.
$19^3 \times 22^4$

48'-0"

© design basics inc.

1580 Finished Sq. Ft.

ORDER DIRECT
7:00-6:00 Mon.-Fri. CST
800-947-PLAN

design basics inc
HOME PLAN DESIGN SERVICE

LGS2290-16 Monterey

PRICE CODE

▶ High quality, erasable, reproducible vellums
▶ Shipped via 2nd day air within the continental U.S.

• brick and stucco enhance the dramatic front elevation showcased by sleek lines and decorative windows
• inviting entry with view into great room is enhanced by arched window and plant shelves above

• fireplace in great room framed by sunny windows with transoms above
• bayed window dining room nestled between great room and superb kitchen/breakfast area

• design of sleeping areas places buffer between secondary bedrooms and master suite
• peaceful master suite enjoys vaulted ceiling, roomy walk-in closet and sunlit master bath with dual lavs and whirlpool

Rear Elevation

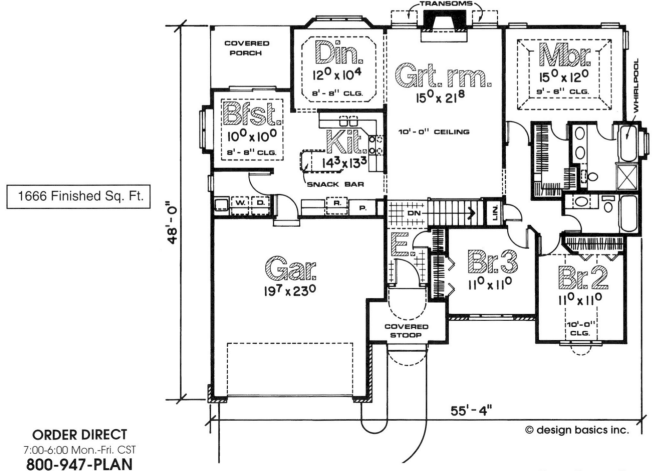

1666 Finished Sq. Ft.

ORDER DIRECT
7:00-6:00 Mon.-Fri. CST
800-947-PLAN

© design basics inc.

design basics inc.®
HOME PLAN DESIGN SERVICE

LGS2355-<u>17</u> Waverly
PRICE CODE

- appealing finishing details and inviting covered porch on elevation
- formal dining room off entry features 10-foot walls and elegant ceiling design
- volume great room with raised hearth fireplace framed by sparkling windows

- comfortable kitchen and bowed dinette area with snack bar, pantry, lazy Susan and access for outdoor pursuits
- two secondary bedrooms convertible to a sun room with French doors from the dinette and an optional den

- bedroom #3 has built-in desk flanked by two closets
- secluded master suite features boxed ceiling, skylit dressing area, his and her lavs with knee space between, corner whirlpool tub and roomy walk-in closet

Rear Elevation

PROMOTIONAL LICENSE

Black and White, Camera-Ready Artwork of the home plan FREE with any plan purchase to assist you in advertising the home.

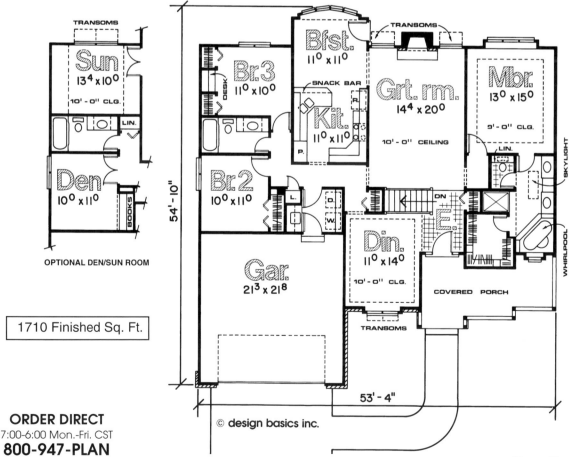

Sun 13⁴ x 10⁰ 10' - 0" CLG.

Den 10⁰ x 11⁰ BOOKS

OPTIONAL DEN/SUN ROOM

TRANSOMS

LIN.

Br. 3 11⁰ x 10⁰ DESK

Br. 2 10⁰ x 11⁰

Bfst. 11⁰ x 11⁰ SNACK BAR

Kit. 11⁰ x 11⁰ P.

Grt. rm. 14⁴ x 20⁰ 10' - 0" CEILING

TRANSOMS

Mbr. 13⁰ x 15⁰ 9' - 0" CLG.

LIN. SKYLIGHT

WHIRLPOOL

Gar. 21³ x 21⁸

Din. 11⁰ x 14⁰ 10' - 0" CLG.

DN

COVERED PORCH

TRANSOMS

54' - 10"

53' - 4"

1710 Finished Sq. Ft.

© design basics inc.

design basics inc.
HOME PLAN DESIGN SERVICE

PRICE CODE
LGS3006-18 Grayson

▶ High quality, erasable, reproducible vellums
▶ Shipped via 2nd day air within the continental U.S.

- beautiful columns and arched transoms are focal points of this ranch home elevation
- 10-foot entry has formal views of volume dining room and great room featuring brick fireplace and arched windows
- large island kitchen offers angled range and pantry
- sunny breakfast room has atrium door to back yard
- garage with built-in shelves accesses home through efficient laundry room
- separate bedroom wings provide optimum privacy
- private master suite includes whirlpool bath with sloped ceiling, plant shelf above dual lavs and large walk-in closet

Rear Elevation

ALL DESIGN BASICS PLANS HAVE BEEN REGISTERED
ORIGINAL © **DRAFT**
WITH THE U.S. COPYRIGHT OFFICE

1806 Finished Sq. Ft.

Bfst. 11⁴ x 11⁴

Grt. rm. 15⁰ x 20⁰
10'-0" CEILING

Br. 2 11⁰ x 11⁰

Kit. 12¹⁰ x 12⁰

Br. 3 11⁰ x 11⁰

LIN.
W.
D.

SHELVES

Din. 11⁰ x 14⁰
10'-0" CLG.

E.

Mbr. 14⁰ x 15⁰
10'-0" CLG.

WHIRLPOOL

Gar. 23⁴ x 22⁴

COVERED PORCH

56' - 0"

© design basics inc.   55' - 4"

ORDER DIRECT
7:00-6:00 Mon.-Fri. CST
800-947-PLAN

VISA MasterCard AMERICAN EXPRESS Cards DISCOVER NOVUS

design basics inc.
HOME PLAN DESIGN SERVICE

LGS1559-18 Bancroft

PRICE CODE

- front porch features repeating arches
- hard-surfaced traffic ways
- 10-foot ceilings through entry, great room and staircase
- sunny dinette with planning desk and bayed window

- roomy kitchen with pantry, 2 lazy Susans and snack bar shares see-thru fireplace with great room
- wet bar/servery between dinette and great room
- oversized garage with plenty of storage

- volume master bedroom with arched window
- master bath has walk-in closet, his and her vanities and corner whirlpool tub with windows above
- Hollywood bath for secondary bedrooms

Rear Elevation

Parade Home Package
available for all plans

1808 Finished Sq. Ft.

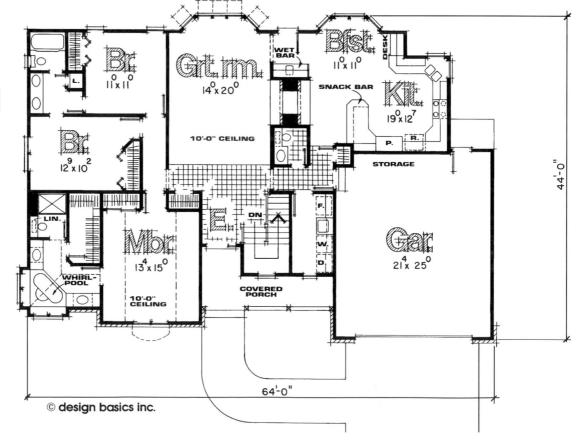

ORDER DIRECT
7:00-6:00 Mon.-Fri. CST
800-947-PLAN

© design basics inc.

design basics inc.
HOME PLAN DESIGN SERVICE

LGS2461-18 Shawnee

PRICE CODE 18

Gold Seal HOME PLANS

- ▶ High quality, erasable, reproducible vellums
- ▶ Shipped via 2nd day air within the continental U.S.

- appealing roofline and covered porch with repeating arches
- kitchen/dinette area includes bayed eating area, wrapping counters, desk, island and wet bar/servery for entertaining ease

- impactful 10-foot-high entry
- decorative hutch space in dining room
- windows frame fireplace in great room
- laundry/mud room with sink and extra counter space

- bedroom #2 can be utilized as an optional den
- master suite enjoys decorative boxed ceiling and elegant windows to the rear, dual lavs, walk-in closet, whirlpool and cedar-lined window seat for storage

Rear Elevation

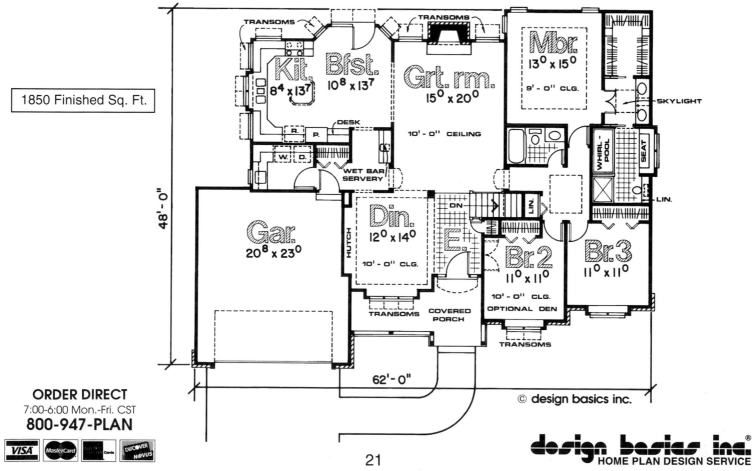

1850 Finished Sq. Ft.

48'-0"

62'-0"

© design basics inc.

ORDER DIRECT
7:00-6:00 Mon.-Fri. CST

800-947-PLAN

VISA   MasterCard   Cards   DISCOVER NOVUS

design basics inc.
HOME PLAN DESIGN SERVICE

21

LGS1748-19 Sinclair

PRICE CODE

Gold Seal ™
HOME PLANS

▶ High quality, erasable, reproducible vellums
▶ Shipped via 2nd day air within the continental U.S.

- alternate elevation at no extra cost
- 10-foot ceiling at entry and great room
- beautiful arched dining room window and detailed ceiling to 12 foot high
- see-thru fireplace seen from entry
- hearth area open to kitchen

- gourmet kitchen caters to the serious cook with corner sink, pantry, snack bar and adjacent eating area
- add French doors to bedroom adjacent to great room for optional den, remove closet for built-in bookcase

- master bedroom with vaulted ceiling and corner windows
- complete master bath area with skylight, whirlpool, his and her vanity and large walk-in closet

Rear Elevation

Alternate Elevation At No Extra Cost

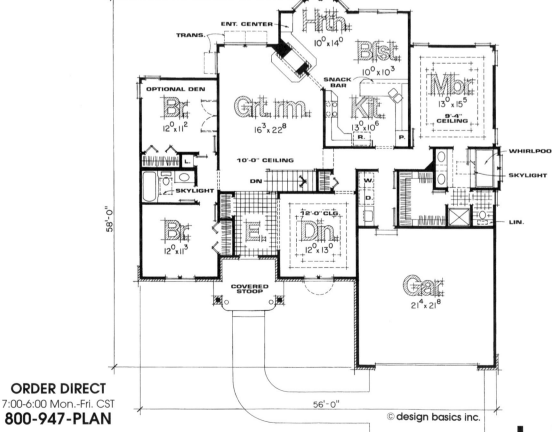

1911 Finished Sq. Ft.

ORDER DIRECT

7:00-6:00 Mon.-Fri. CST

800-947-PLAN

© design basics inc.

design basics inc. ®
HOME PLAN DESIGN SERVICE

LGS3031-19 Jonesville

PRICE CODE

- special detailing and front porch create sophisticated elevation
- dramatic formal dining room open to 10-foot-tall entry
- living room has large windows and cased opening to family room

- family room open to kitchen and breakfast area provides great atmosphere for informal gatherings
- breakfast area with 2 pantries and built-in desk complements island kitchen
- laundry has access to covered porch

- secondary bedrooms off entry share hall bath
- French doors open to master suite, enhanced by private back yard access and whirlpool bath with spacious closet and dual lavs

Rear Elevation

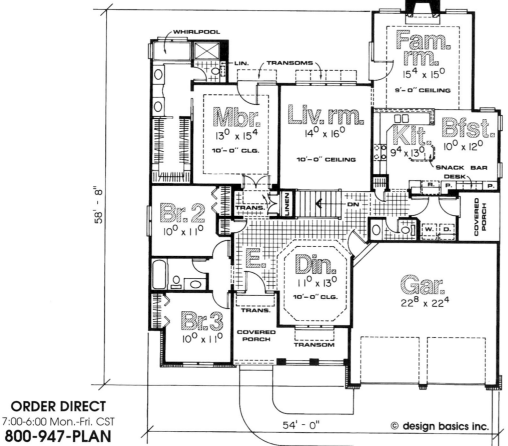

WHIRLPOOL

LIN. TRANSOMS

Fam. rm.
15⁴ x 15⁰
9'-0" CEILING

Mbr.
13⁰ x 15⁴
10'-0" CLG.

Liv. rm.
14⁰ x 16⁰
10'-0" CEILING

Kit.
9⁴ x 13⁰

Bfst.
10⁰ x 12⁰

SNACK BAR
DESK

Br. 2
10⁰ x 11⁰

TRANS.

LINEN

DN

R.   P.   P.

COVERED PORCH

W. D.

58' - 8"

E.

Din.
11⁰ x 13⁰
10'-0" CLG.

Gar.
22⁸ x 22⁴

Br. 3
10⁰ x 11⁰

TRANS.

COVERED PORCH

TRANSOM

1978 Finished Sq. Ft.

54' - 0"

© design basics inc.

LGS3139-20 Foxboro

PRICE CODE

▶ **High quality, erasable, reproducible vellums**
▶ **Shipped via 2nd day air within the continental U.S.**

- universally designed home
- arched details decorate this quaint ranch style home
- formal entry presents great room with brick fireplace, transoms and 10-foot-high ceiling

- sizeable breakfast area shines with bayed windows and access to screen porch
- spacious peninsula kitchen contains snack bar, pantry and pull-out shelf for extra counter space

- master suite features bayed window, roomy closet, dressing area, dual lavs, whirlpool bath and oversized shower
- bedroom #3 has window seat, 9-foot-high ceiling and can be an optional den
- stairs to basement have elevator option

Rear Elevation

Parade Home Package *available for all plans*

2053 Finished Sq. Ft.

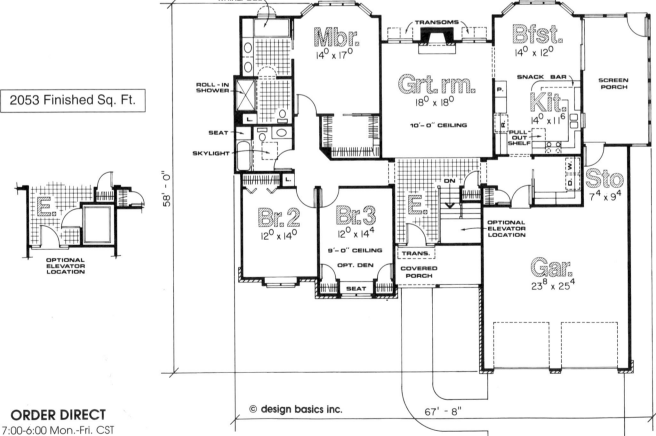

© design basics inc.

67' - 8"

58' - 0"

OPTIONAL ELEVATOR LOCATION

ORDER DIRECT
7:00-6:00 Mon.-Fri. CST
800-947-PLAN

LGS2222-20 Plainview

PRICE CODE

► High quality, erasable, reproducible vellums
► Shipped via 2nd day air within the continental U.S.

Gold Seal
HOME PLANS™

- elegant covered veranda at entry
- 10-foot or higher ceilings in entry and great room
- spectacular window out the back highlights great room
- 3-sided fireplace serves gathering areas

- abundance of windows throughout
- pantry, planning desk, and island counter with snack bar in kitchen
- convenient powder bath location
- garage with extra storage space accesses home through laundry/mud room

- den becomes third bedroom with optional door location
- irresistible master suite with private covered deck and pampering dressing area with whirlpool and large walk-in closet

Rear Elevation

2068 Finished Sq. Ft.

Covered Deck

Mbr. 15⁰ x 13⁴ — 9'-0" CLG.

Grt. rm. 15⁰ x 20⁰ — 10'-8" CEILING

Hrth. 10⁸ x 10⁴

Bfst. 12⁸ x 11¹⁰ — 8'-8" CLG.

Kit. 12⁸ x 11⁴

SNACK BAR

DRESSER

W/P

GLASS BLOCK

LIN.

DESK

R.

L.

P.

Br.2 11⁰ x 11⁰

Den 11³ x 14² — 10'-0" CEILING — OPT. BEDROOM

Din. 11⁴ x 14⁰ — 10'-0" CLG.

W. D.

STORAGE

Gar. 22⁰ x 21⁴

DN

UP

COVERED VERANDA

56'-0"

66'-0"

© design basics inc.

25

design basics inc.®
HOME PLAN DESIGN SERVICE

PRICE CODE

LGS3196-21 Galloway

Gold Seal™ HOME PLANS

- High quality, erasable, reproducible vellums
- Shipped via 2nd day air within the continental U.S.

- stucco and brick details complement this ranch style home
- ceiling details enhance formal dining room
- formal living room has view of screen porch through spacious windows
- family room is warmed by fireplace and provides access to screen porch
- breakfast/kitchen area boasts broom closet, snack bar, pantry and lazy Susans
- master suite features large walk-in closet, dual lavs and whirlpool bath
- secondary bedrooms share convenient hall bath

Rear Elevation

2120 Finished Sq. Ft.

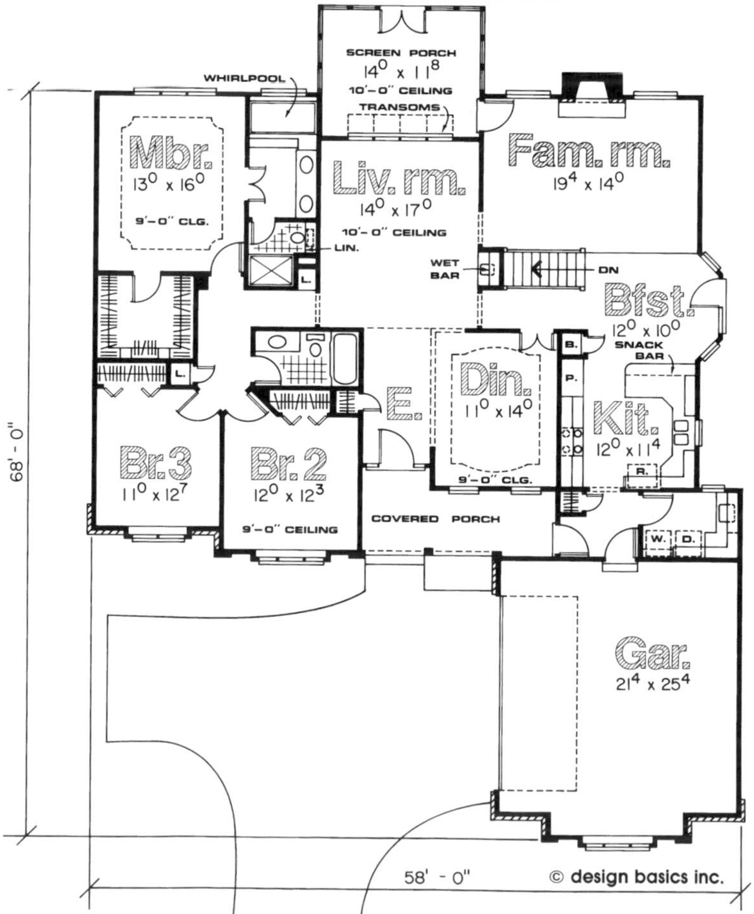

ORDER DIRECT
7:00-6:00 Mon.-Fri. CST
800-947-PLAN

VISA MasterCard American Express Cards DISCOVER NOVUS

design basics inc.® HOME PLAN DESIGN SERVICE

LGS1689-21 Newman

PRICE CODE

Gold Seal
HOME PLANS™

- many lot arrangement possibilities
- visually open plan
- diagonal views give expansive look
- arched ceiling at entry
- entry views volume great room with fireplace flanked by windows

- stunning dining room
- island kitchen with snack bar, desk and walk-in pantry adjoins bayed breakfast area
- 3-car garage with extra storage space accesses home through mud/laundry room

- secondary bedrooms share hall bath
- double doors lead to master bedroom with tiered ceiling and access to covered deck
- romantic master bath with whirlpool, double vanity and walk-in closet

Rear Elevation

Parade Home Package
available for all plans

2133 Finished Sq. Ft.

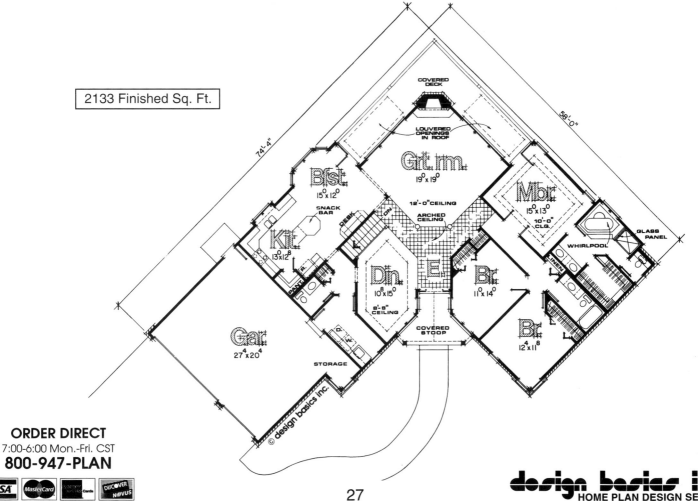

design basics inc.
HOME PLAN DESIGN SERVICE

LGS3005-21 Wrenwood

PRICE CODE

▶ High quality, erasable, reproducible vellums
▶ Shipped via 2nd day air within the continental U.S.

Gold Seal ™
HOME PLANS

- brick columns and tall gabled entry create prominent elevation
- bright 12-foot-tall entry views large great room with entertainment center, brick fireplace and direct access to dining room and kitchen

- gourmet island kitchen with wet bar, wrapping pantry and snack bar is well-integrated with bayed breakfast area and dining room
- utility corridor has laundry room to one side and computer center to the other

- 3-car garage has sunlit shop area
- secondary bedrooms share large bath
- bedroom #3 offers versatile den option
- master suite has spacious walk-in closet, lavish whirlpool bath and 10-foot ceiling in bedroom

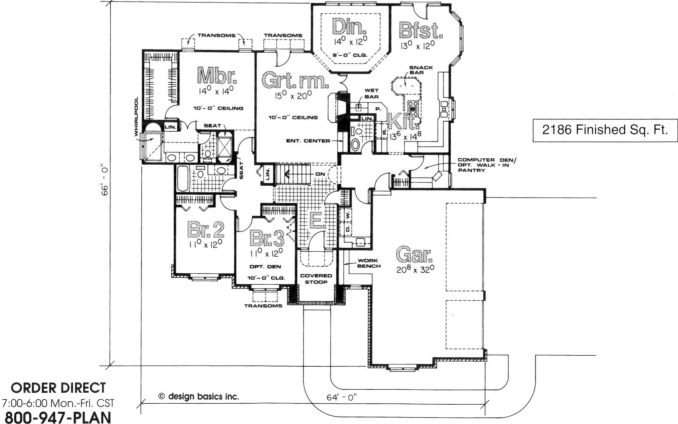

Rear Elevation

ALL PLANS *Customizable*

2186 Finished Sq. Ft.

ORDER DIRECT
7:00-6:00 Mon.-Fri. CST
800-947-PLAN

design basics inc.
HOME PLAN DESIGN SERVICE

LGS3058-23 Montgomery

PRICE CODE **23**

Gold Seal™
HOME PLANS

- ▶ High quality, erasable, reproducible vellums
- ▶ Shipped via 2nd day air within the continental U.S.

- great details on front porch add curb appeal to this ranch home
- 10-foot ceiling shared by entry, great room and dining room accentuate openness
- great room highlighted by arched windows and pass thru wet bar/buffet

- arched openings create special entrances to utility and bedroom wings
- well planned kitchen features walk-in pantry and wrapping island snack bar
- ample laundry room has desirable access to covered service porch

- corridor design offers privacy between master suite and secondary bedrooms
- his and her walk-in closets, large dressing area and separate shower and whirlpool space in bath produce stylish master suite

G. MacDonald

Rear Elevation

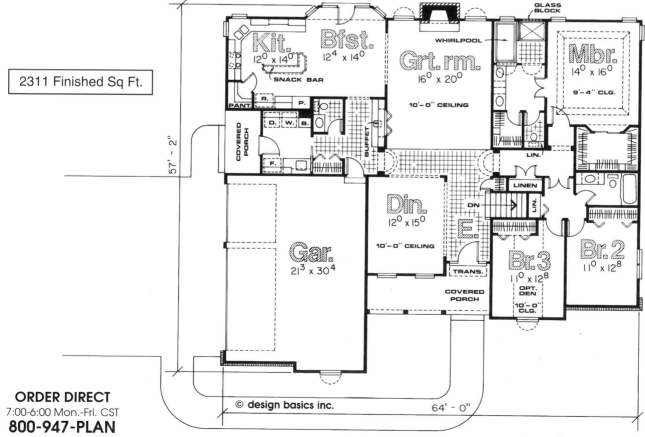

2311 Finished Sq Ft.

ORDER DIRECT
7:00-6:00 Mon.-Fri. CST
800-947-PLAN

© design basics inc.

design basics inc.®
HOME PLAN DESIGN SERVICE

LGS3018-29 Shiloh

PRICE CODE

▶ **High quality, erasable, reproducible vellums**
▶ **Shipped via 2nd day air within the continental U.S.**

- spectacular front porch commands plantation style elevation
- formal dining room captures elegant views of arched openings to great room
- gourmet kitchen features 2 pantries and wrapping island snack bar

- gathering room with cathedral ceiling, brick fireplace and entertainment center has useful service porch entrance
- private access to arbor and secluded work space highlight spacious master bedroom

- grand master bath features large oval whirlpool tub, his and her vanities and entrance to extensive walk-in closet
- bedroom #2 can become private study off master bedroom while bedroom #4 easily converts to optional den

Rear Elevation

ALL PLANS *Customizable*

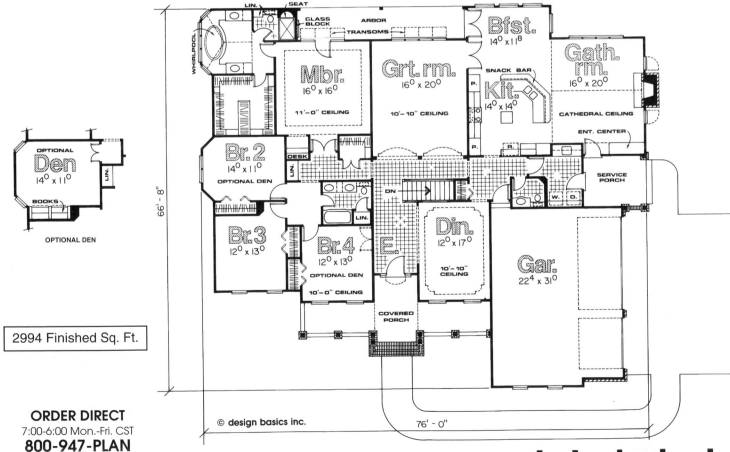

2994 Finished Sq. Ft.

ORDER DIRECT
7:00-6:00 Mon.-Fri. CST
800-947-PLAN

© design basics inc.

design basics inc.
HOME PLAN DESIGN SERVICE

1 ¹/₂ STORY HOMES

LGS3123-15 Bethany

PRICE CODE

▶ **High quality, erasable, reproducible vellums**
▶ **Shipped via 2nd day air within the continental U.S.**

- charming country style elevation has wrapping porch and oval accents
- spacious great room, directly accessible from 2-story entry and breakfast area with bowed window

- angled wall adds drama to peninsula kitchen and creates private entry to master suite
- master suite contains boxed 9-foot ceiling, compartmented whirlpool bath and spacious walk-in closet

- second level balcony overlooks U-stairs and entry
- twin linen closets just outside upstairs bedrooms serve compartmented bath with natural light

Rear Elevation

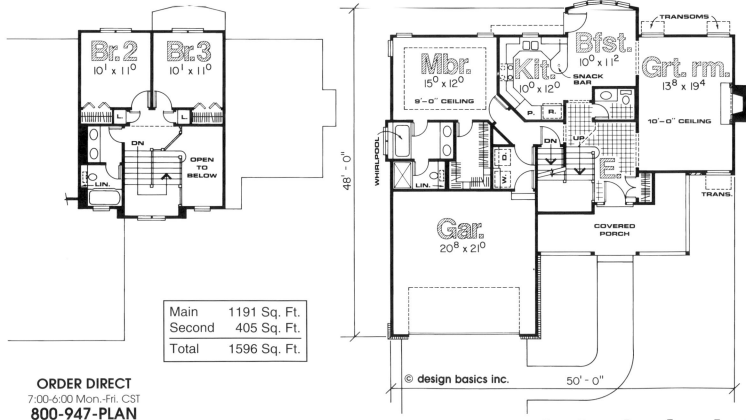

Main	1191 Sq. Ft.
Second	405 Sq. Ft.
Total	1596 Sq. Ft.

ORDER DIRECT
7:00-6:00 Mon.-Fri. CST
800-947-PLAN

VISA MasterCard American Express Cards DISCOVER NOVUS

32

design basics inc.
HOME PLAN DESIGN SERVICE

LGS2578-16 Kaiser

PRICE CODE

> ▸ High quality, erasable, reproducible vellums
> ▸ Shipped via 2nd day air within the continental U.S.

- suited for narrow lots, this home demonstrates design efficiency
- paladian arch supported by stylish columns shelters entry stoop
- off entry, wide-cased opening leads to bright formal dining room

- volume entry is accented by glass blocks that spotlight decorator plant shelf above guest coat closet
- great room with its 10'-8" ceiling, full wall of windows and brick fireplace create inviting atmosphere

- dinette achieves light, open sensation with its 10-foot ceiling and large windows
- master bedroom, with its 9-foot boxed ceiling and expansive window area, affords maximum privacy

Rear Elevation

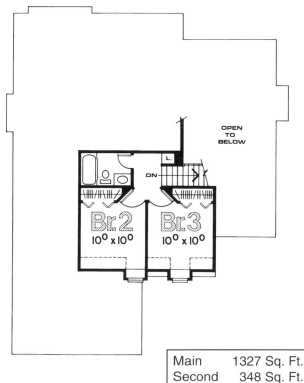

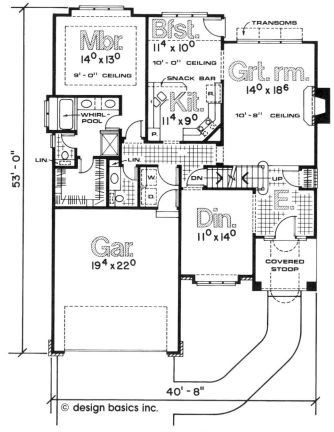

Main	1327 Sq. Ft.
Second	348 Sq. Ft.
Total	1675 Sq. Ft.

© design basics inc.

ORDER DIRECT
7:00-6:00 Mon.-Fri. CST
800-947-PLAN

design basics inc.
HOME PLAN DESIGN SERVICE

LGS3089-17 Parnell
PRICE CODE 17

- High quality, erasable, reproducible vellums
- Shipped via 2nd day air within the continental U.S.

- 2 story entry with plant shelf above door introduces formal dining room and sun-filled great room
- large breakfast area shares snack bar with peninsula kitchen

- generous laundry room features window overlooking front porch
- French doors open to master suite including great whirlpool bath with arched opening, large plant shelf and walk-in closet

- upstairs, well-planned corridor accesses secondary bedrooms, hall bath and popular storage area
- side-load garage boasts extra storage space

Rear Elevation

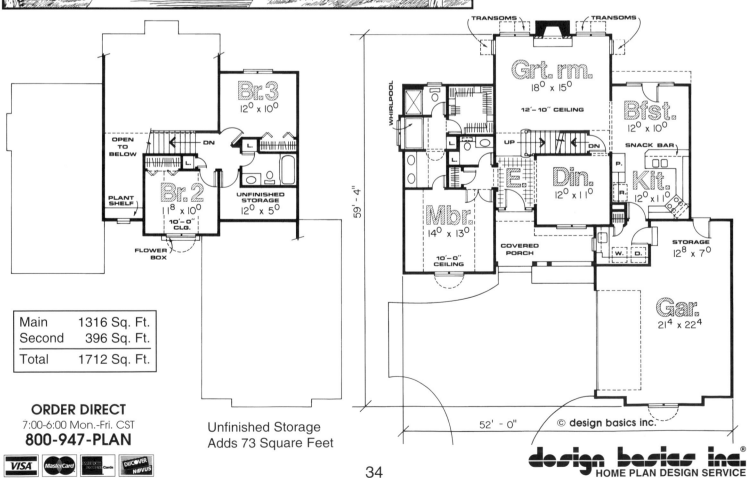

Main	1316 Sq. Ft.
Second	396 Sq. Ft.
Total	1712 Sq. Ft.

ORDER DIRECT
7:00-6:00 Mon.-Fri. CST
800-947-PLAN

VISA MasterCard DISCOVER NOVUS

Unfinished Storage
Adds 73 Square Feet

© design basics inc.

design basics inc.®
HOME PLAN DESIGN SERVICE

34

LGS2281-17 Ingram
PRICE CODE

▶ **High quality, erasable, reproducible vellums**
▶ **Shipped via 2nd day air within the continental U.S.**

- inviting covered porch
- elegant bayed window in formal dining room off entry
- beautiful fireplace with windows showcased in large great room

- bright bayed dinette
- kitchen with window above sink, pantry and snack bar
- utility entrance through garage
- additional storage in garage

- master suite features tiered ceiling, corner windows and luxurious dressing area with double lav vanity, 2 closets and corner whirlpool under windows
- convenient hall bath services secondary bedrooms

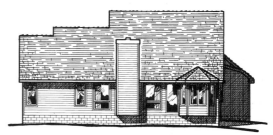

Rear Elevation

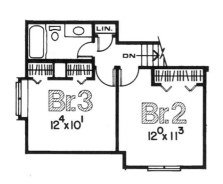

Main	1348 Sq. Ft.
Second	430 Sq. Ft.
Total	1778 Sq. Ft.

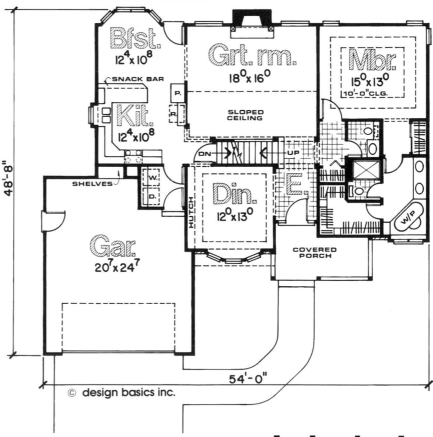

48'-8"

54'-0"

© design basics inc.

ORDER DIRECT
7:00-6:00 Mon.-Fri. CST
800-947-PLAN

design basics inc.
HOME PLAN DESIGN SERVICE

LGS3385-17 Brittany

PRICE CODE

- exciting curb appeal enhanced by long front porch and gingerbread accents
- transom windows and 11'-0" ceiling adorn great room
- interesting angles and unique snack bar highlight unforgettable kitchen
- bowed breakfast area links great room and kitchen
- master bedroom has 9'-0" boxed ceiling, large walk-in closet and pampering bath
- centrally located main floor powder room
- U-shaped staircase leads to second floor where balcony views entry below
- three secondary bedrooms served by full bath and two hall linen closets

Rear Elevation

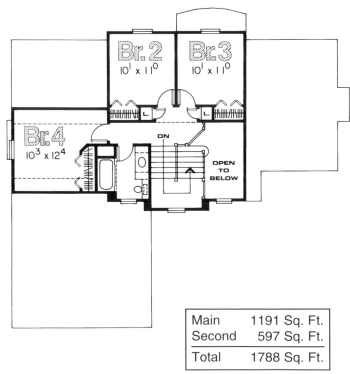

Main	1191 Sq. Ft.
Second	597 Sq. Ft.
Total	1788 Sq. Ft.

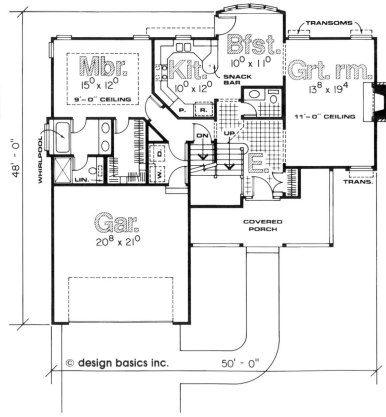

© design basics inc.

50' - 0"

ORDER DIRECT
7:00-6:00 Mon.-Fri. CST
800-947-PLAN

36

design basics inc.
HOME PLAN DESIGN SERVICE

PRICE CODE

LGS2236-18 Bermier

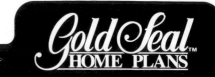

- ▶ High quality, erasable, reproducible vellums
- ▶ Shipped via 2nd day air within the continental U.S.

Gold Seal™ HOME PLANS

- inviting covered front porch
- formal dining room with large boxed window seen from entry
- views into great room reveal handsome fireplace and tall windows
- snack bar, pantry, 2 lazy Susans and desk for kitchen/dinette area
- closet at service entry through garage
- window in laundry room
- large boxed window in volume master bedroom
- skylit master dressing area with double vanity, whirlpool, compartmented stool and shower
- upstairs, fourth bedroom has volume ceiling above beautiful arched window

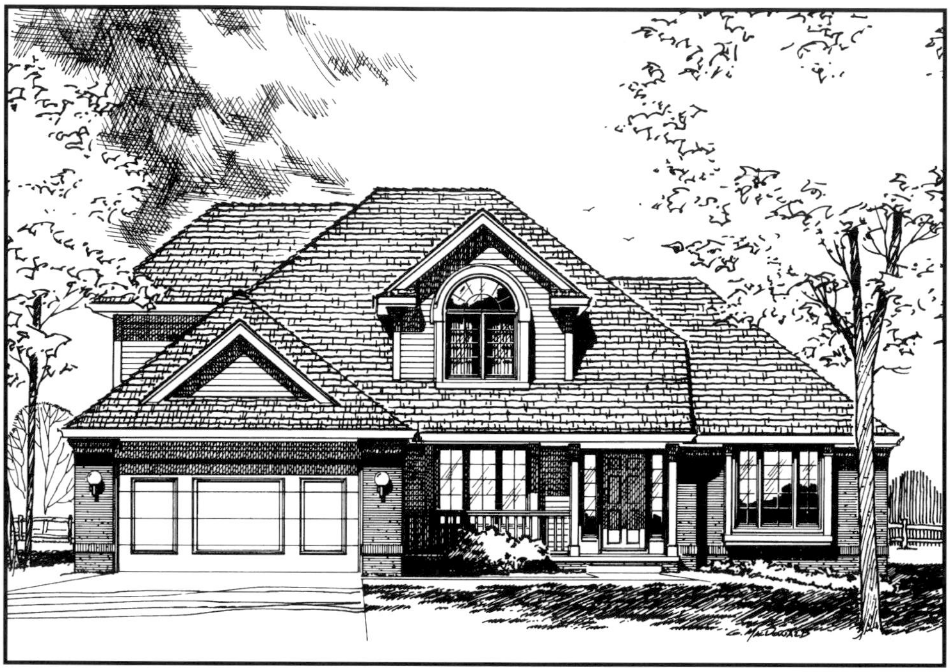

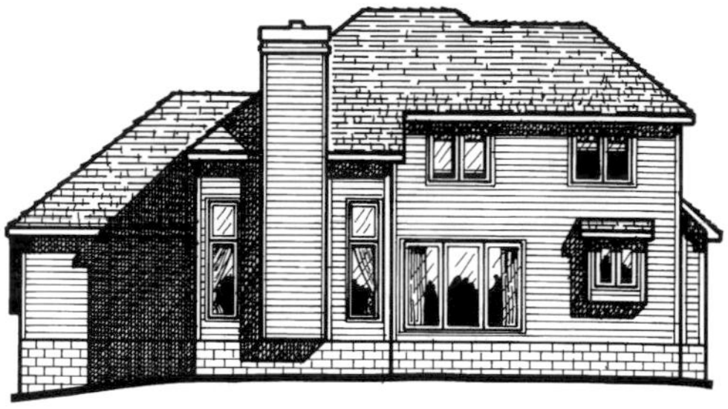

Rear Elevation

Unfinished Storage
Adds 141 Sq. Ft.

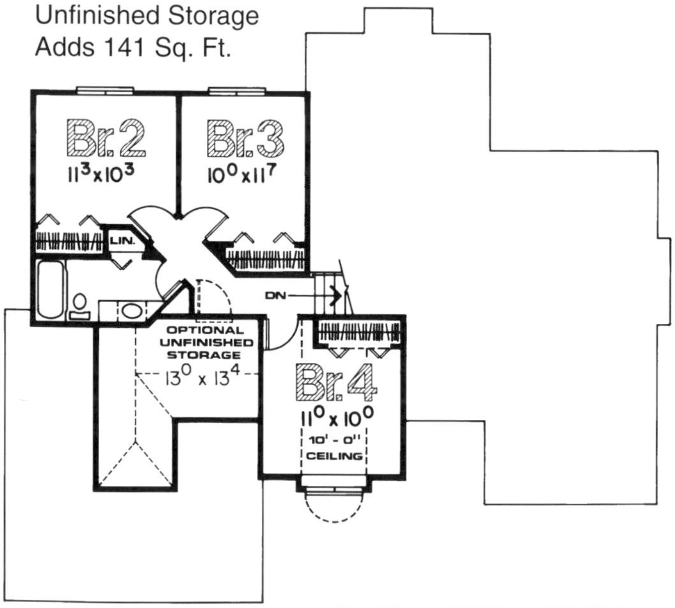

Br.2
11³x10³
Br.3
10⁰x11⁷
LIN.
DN
OPTIONAL UNFINISHED STORAGE
13⁰ x 13⁴
Br.4
11⁰x10⁰
10' - 0" CEILING

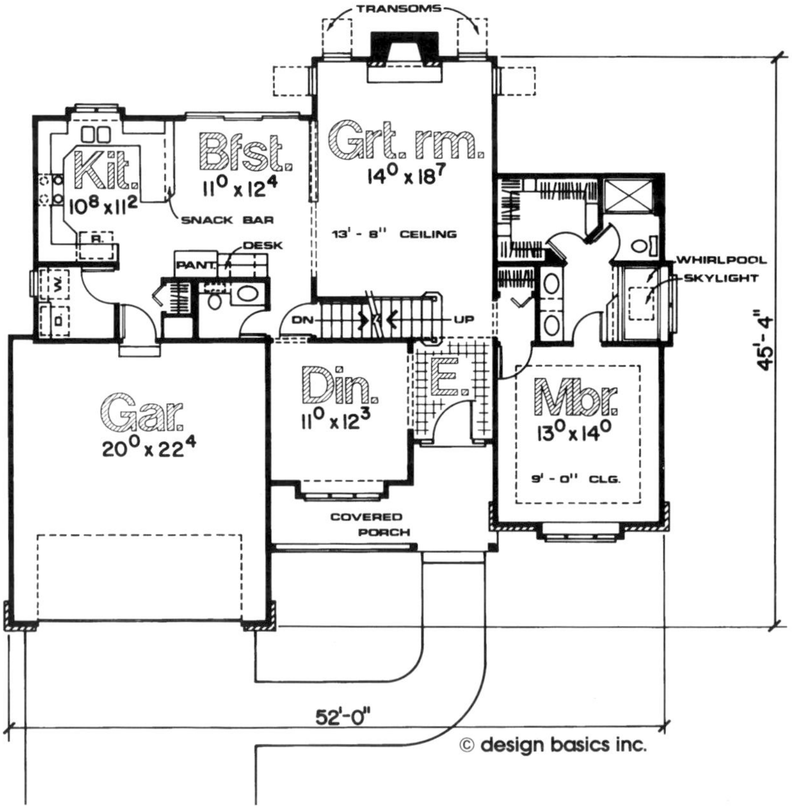

TRANSOMS
Kit.
10⁸x11²
Bfst.
11⁰x12⁴
Grt. rm.
14⁰x18⁷
13' - 8" CEILING
SNACK BAR
DESK
PANT.
W
D
R
DN
UP
WHIRLPOOL
SKYLIGHT
Gar.
20⁰x22⁴
Din.
11⁰x12³
E.
Mbr.
13⁰x14⁰
9' - 0" CLG.
COVERED PORCH
45'-4"
52'-0"

Main	1297 Sq. Ft.
Second	558 Sq. Ft.
Total	1855 Sq. Ft.

© design basics inc.

ORDER DIRECT
7:00-6:00 Mon.-Fri. CST
800-947-PLAN

design basics inc.®
HOME PLAN DESIGN SERVICE

LGS1867-19 Langley

► High quality, erasable, reproducible vellums
► Shipped via 2nd day air within the continental U.S.

- sleek lines coupled with impressive detailing enhance elevation
- entry opens into volume great room with fireplace flanked by cheerful windows
- dining room off great room offers entertaining options
- kitchen and breakfast area has cooktop in island and access to covered patio
- bridge overlook on second level
- secondary bedrooms share compartmented bath with dual lavs
- master bedroom secluded on first level includes decorative ceiling and bright boxed window
- luxurious master bath has two closets, separate wet and dry areas, dual lavs and whirlpool tub

Rear Elevation

PROMOTIONAL LICENSE • PROMOTIONAL LICENSE • PROMOTIONAL LICENSE • PROMOTIONAL LICENSE •

Black and White, Camera-Ready Artwork of the home plan FREE with any plan purchase to assist you in advertising the home.

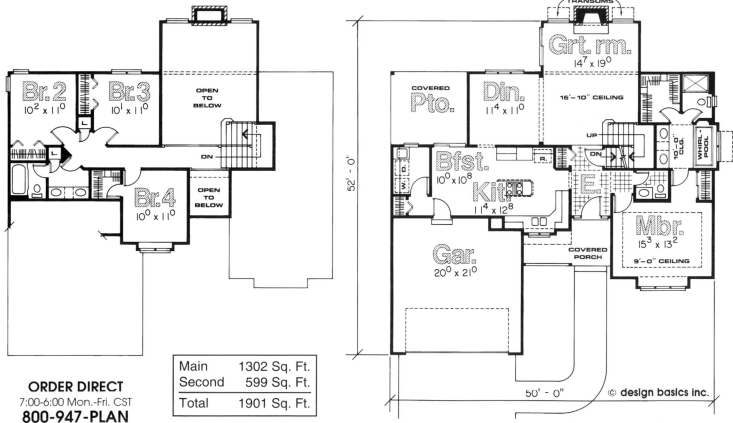

Main	1302 Sq. Ft.
Second	599 Sq. Ft.
Total	1901 Sq. Ft.

ORDER DIRECT

7:00-6:00 Mon.-Fri. CST

800-947-PLAN

design basics inc.
HOME PLAN DESIGN SERVICE

LGS1330-18 Trenton

PRICE CODE

Gold Seal™
HOME PLANS

- entry open to formal dining room with hutch space
- volume great room with see-thru fireplace flooded with natural light from large windows to the back

- hearth kitchen area with bayed dinette, has see-thru fireplace, planning desk and large corner walk-in pantry
- conveniently located powder bath
- main floor mud/laundry area with coat closet and laundry sink

- centralized bathroom convenient for secondary bedrooms
- master suite with sloped ceiling includes walk-in closet, double vanity and corner whirlpool tub

Rear Elevation

Main	1421 Sq. Ft.
Second	448 Sq. Ft.
Total	1869 Sq. Ft.

© design basics inc.

design basics inc.®
HOME PLAN DESIGN SERVICE

LGS3063-**19** Taylor
PRICE CODE

- country style elevation highlighted by detailed porch and brick accents
- formal dining room proudly welcomes guests at entry
- well-integrated family room, kitchen and breakfast area accommodate many family activities
- master suite contains 10-foot-high ceilings while angled doors in the whirlpool bath add drama
- 3 secondary bedrooms share roomy hall bath serviced by large linen
- ample unfinished storage is a great feature in this 1½ story home

Rear Elevation

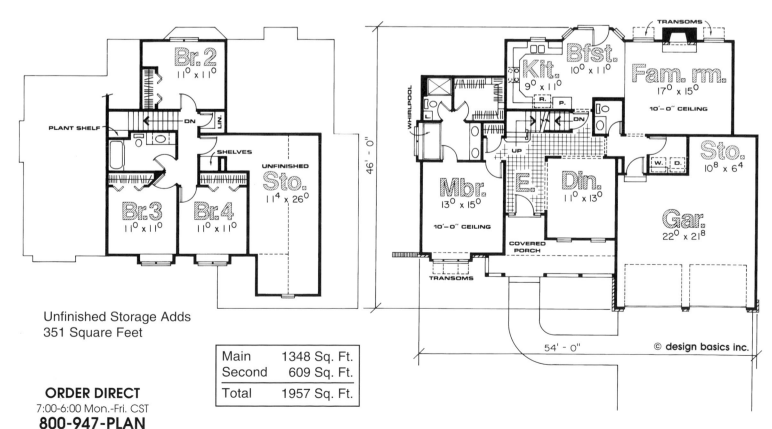

Unfinished Storage Adds
351 Square Feet

Main	1348 Sq. Ft.
Second	609 Sq. Ft.
Total	1957 Sq. Ft.

ORDER DIRECT
7:00-6:00 Mon.-Fri. CST
800-947-PLAN

design basics inc.
HOME PLAN DESIGN SERVICE

LGS3556-19 Pottersville

PRICE CODE

- comfortable elevation reveals its family style
- wrapping front porch
- oak entry showcases U-shaped staircase
- dining room expands entry and has intricate ceiling detail

- French doors lead to island kitchen flooded with light from bayed breakfast area
- family room with cathedral ceiling and fireplace also benefits from snack bar

- master bedroom has volume ceiling and romantic bath with whirlpool
- laundry room offers soaking sink
- large garage with handy storage closet

Rear Elevation

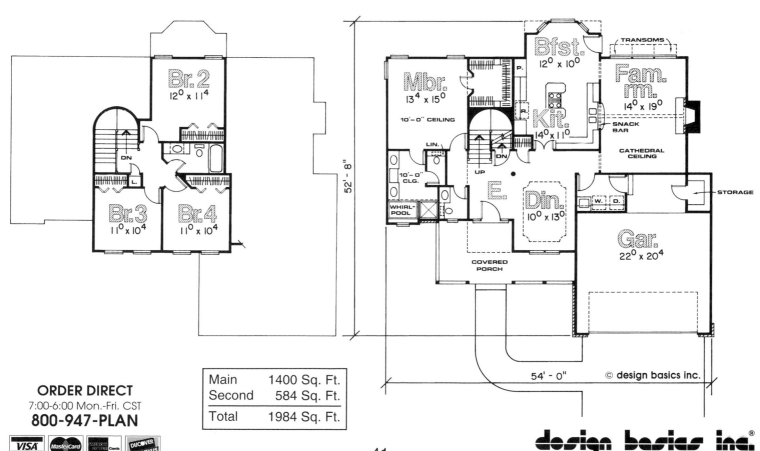

52' - 8"

54' - 0"

© design basics inc.

Main	1400 Sq. Ft.
Second	584 Sq. Ft.
Total	1984 Sq. Ft.

design basics inc.
HOME PLAN DESIGN SERVICE

LGS1380-**19** Paterson
PRICE CODE

► High quality, erasable, reproducible vellums
► Shipped via 2nd day air within the continental U.S.

- inviting front porch welcomes guests
- hard-surfaced entryway is open to formal dining room with hutch space
- volume great room with generous windows and cozy, see-thru fireplace is open to entry

- hearth kitchen with bayed breakfast area and large planning desk
- main floor laundry area with coat closet and laundry sink doubles as mud entry from garage

- elegant sloped ceiling in master suite with pampering bath which includes double vanity, walk-in closet and window above the whirlpool tub
- future expansion possible over garage with access off hall

Rear Elevation

ORDER DIRECT
7:00-6:00 Mon.-Fri. CST

800-947-PLAN

VISA · MasterCard · American Express Cards · DISCOVER NOVUS

Main	1421 Sq. Ft.
Second	578 Sq. Ft.
Total	1999 Sq. Ft.

design basics inc.
HOME PLAN DESIGN SERVICE

LGS3381-20 Amanda

PRICE CODE

▶ **High quality, erasable, reproducible vellums**
▶ **Shipped via 2nd day air within the continental U.S.**

- traditional features enhance cozy appeal
- dining room with dropped perimeter ceiling and bayed windows offers perfect view of refinement
- picture awning windows frame fireplace in great room with 2-story high sloped ceiling

- bayed breakfast area gives view and access to backyard
- kitchen designed to be easily accessible to and from breakfast area, dining room and garage

- secluded master suite provides tiered 10-foot ceiling, corner whirlpool and spacious walk-in closet
- second floor bath serves three roomy bedrooms
- plant shelf garnishes the entry

Rear Elevation

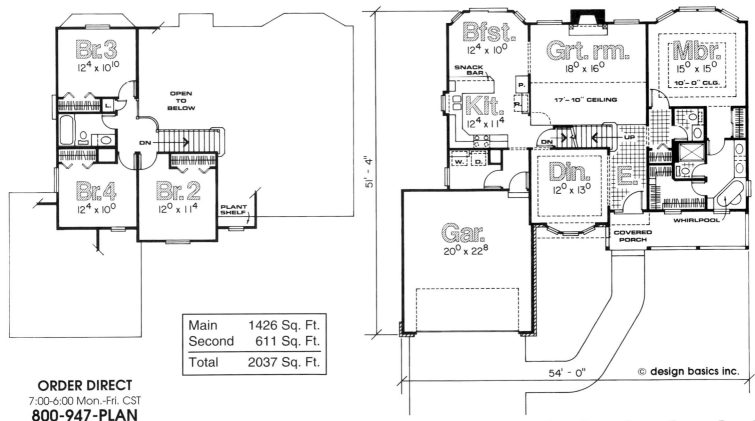

Br. 3 12⁴ x 10¹⁰

Br. 4 12⁴ x 10⁰

Br. 2 12⁰ x 11⁴

OPEN TO BELOW

L.

DN

PLANT SHELF

Bfst. 12⁴ x 10⁰

SNACK BAR

Grt. rm. 18⁰ x 16⁰

17'-10" CEILING

Mbr. 15⁰ x 15⁰
10'-0" CLG.

P.

Kit. 12⁴ x 11⁴

Din. 12⁰ x 13⁰

DN

UP

E.

W. D.

WHIRLPOOL

Gar. 20⁰ x 22⁸

COVERED PORCH

51' - 4"

54' - 0"

© design basics inc.

Main	1426 Sq. Ft.
Second	611 Sq. Ft.
Total	2037 Sq. Ft.

ORDER DIRECT

7:00-6:00 Mon.-Fri. CST

800-947-PLAN

VISA   MasterCard   American Express Cards   DISCOVER NOVUS

design basics inc.®
HOME PLAN DESIGN SERVICE

LGS3064-20 Eldridge

PRICE CODE **20**

► **High quality, erasable, reproducible vellums**
► **Shipped via 2nd day air within the continental U.S.**

- covered porch, bayed window and column details accent this 1½ story home
- entry reveals formal dining room and spacious great room with fireplace and 10-foot-high ceiling
- octagon-shaped breakfast area is enhanced by arched transom windows
- roomy island kitchen features snack bar, lazy Susan and pantry
- master suite offers large walk-in closet, dual lavs, whirlpool bath and shower area
- efficient laundry has convenient access from garage and kitchen
- dual linen closets serve upstairs hall bath with dual lavs

G. MacDonald

Rear Elevation

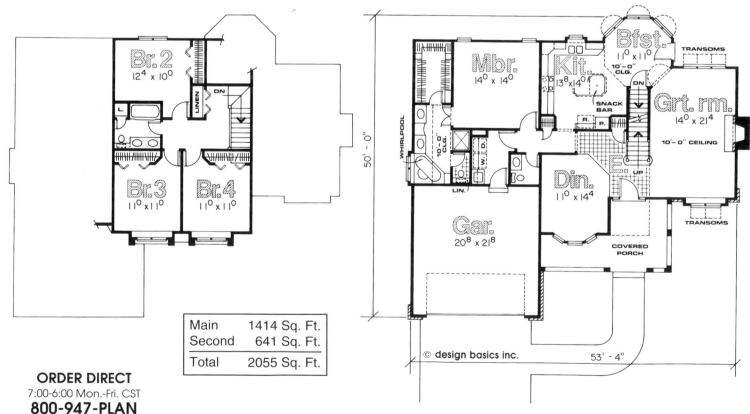

Main	1414 Sq. Ft.
Second	641 Sq. Ft.
Total	2055 Sq. Ft.

© design basics inc.

53' - 4"

ORDER DIRECT
7:00-6:00 Mon.-Fri. CST
800-947-PLAN

44

design basics inc.®
HOME PLAN DESIGN SERVICE

LGS2127-22 Montrose

PRICE CODE **22**

▶ High quality, erasable, reproducible vellums
▶ Shipped via 2nd day air within the continental U.S.

Gold Seal HOME PLANS™

- beautiful bayed window in dining room
- French doors between living room and family room for versatility
- handsome fireplace, entertainment center, bookcase and windows are all a part of the family room

- open dinette adjacent to kitchen with snack bar and pantry
- boxed ceiling in private master bedroom
- skylit master dressing/bath area with decorator plant ledge above, double vanity and whirlpool under window

- angled landing on stairs
- bayed window for bedroom #2
- clothes chute in corridor upstairs
- all second level bedrooms share compartmented hall bath with 2 lavs

Rear Elevation

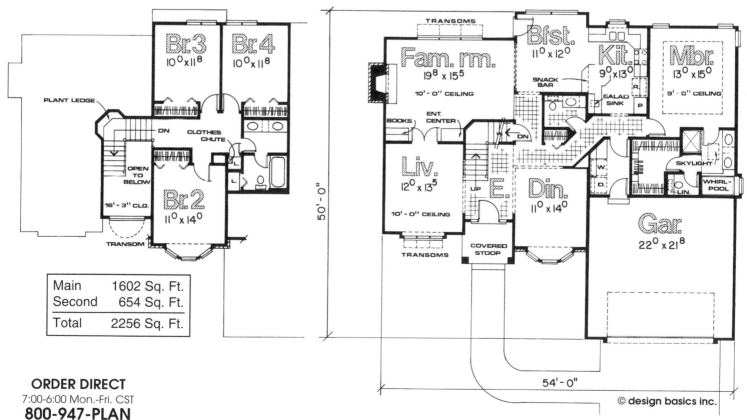

Main	1602 Sq. Ft.
Second	654 Sq. Ft.
Total	2256 Sq. Ft.

ORDER DIRECT
7:00-6:00 Mon.-Fri. CST
800-947-PLAN

© design basics inc.

design basics inc.®
HOME PLAN DESIGN SERVICE

LGS2811-22 Ashville

PRICE CODE

▶ **High quality, erasable, reproducible vellums**
▶ **Shipped via 2nd day air within the continental U.S.**

- wrap-around covered porch and windows create striking front elevation
- entry offers tremendous open view of dining and great room
- fireplace centers on cathedral ceiling which soars to over 16 feet high in great room

- French doors to dinette add formal touch
- kitchen features such amenities as lazy Susan, large food preparation island and ample pantry
- broom closet in laundry room which also serves as mud entry from outside

- double doors access master bedroom with boxed ceiling
- master bath has large whirlpool, dual lavs, makeup vanity and walk-in closet
- walk-in closet is featured in bedroom #3

Rear Elevation

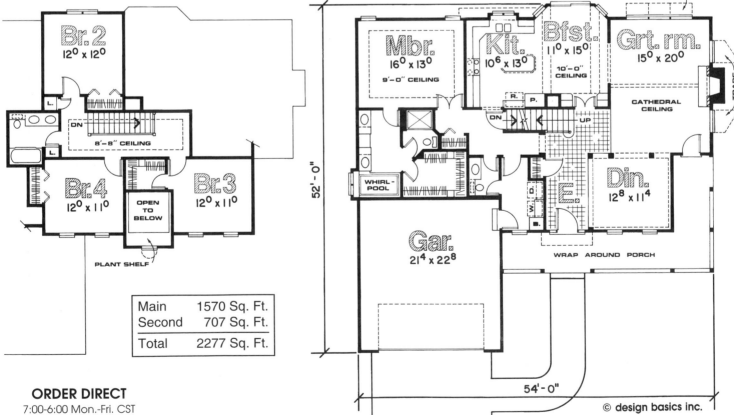

Main	1570 Sq. Ft.
Second	707 Sq. Ft.
Total	**2277 Sq. Ft.**

ORDER DIRECT

7:00-6:00 Mon.-Fri. CST

800-947-PLAN

© design basics inc.

design basics inc.
HOME PLAN DESIGN SERVICE

LGS3020-22 Douglas

► High quality, erasable, reproducible vellums
► Shipped via 2nd day air within the continental U.S.

- soft curves under repeating gables form an inviting elevation
- bayed living room and formal dining room surround beautiful 2-story entry
- peninsula kitchen open to bayed breakfast area has large snack bar

- family room with 16'-10" high sloped ceiling provides relaxed atmosphere for informal get-togethers
- whirlpool bath in master suite is highlighted by a large vanity with dual lavs and make-up counter

- laundry room has access to garage with valuable extra storage space
- upstairs 3 bedrooms share bath with dual lavs
- unfinished storage area and optional loft overlooking family room provide versatility

Rear Elevation

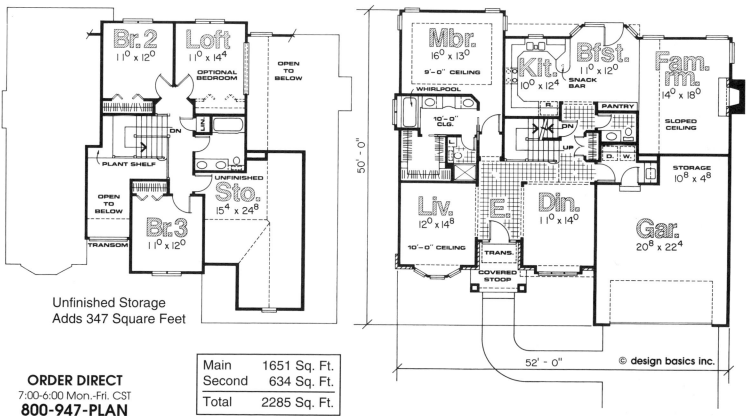

Unfinished Storage
Adds 347 Square Feet

ORDER DIRECT
7:00-6:00 Mon.-Fri. CST
800-947-PLAN

Main	1651 Sq. Ft.
Second	634 Sq. Ft.
Total	2285 Sq. Ft.

design basics inc®
HOME PLAN DESIGN SERVICE

LGS2836-23 Aurora

PRICE CODE

▶ **High quality, erasable, reproducible vellums**
▶ **Shipped via 2nd day air within the continental U.S.**

- brick accents and bright windows highlight this appealing front elevation
- entry provides wide, dramatic view of formal dining room and spacious great room

- extra-tall bowed window complements 13-foot ceiling in great room
- French doors connect delightful sunroom to kitchen/dinette area
- wet bar is conveniently placed to serve dining room and great room

- dramatic master suite with dual bookcases features deluxe bath, abundant windows, outdoor access and generous closet space
- staircase is conveniently located in back of home

Rear Elevation

ALL DESIGN BASICS PLANS HAVE BEEN REGISTERED
ORIGINAL © DRAFT
WITH THE U.S. COPYRIGHT OFFICE

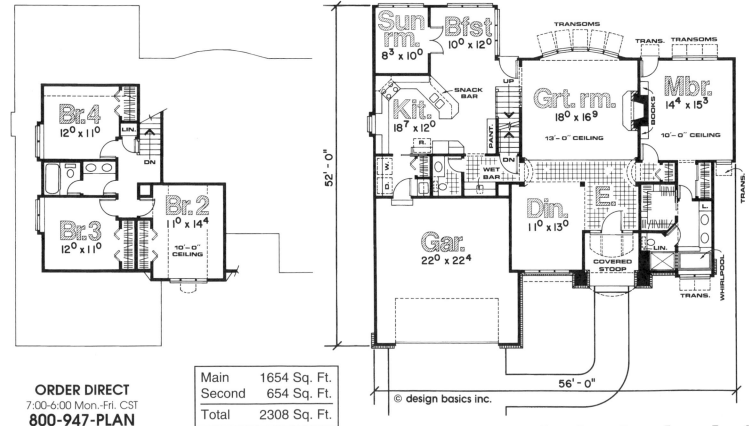

ORDER DIRECT
7:00-6:00 Mon.-Fri. CST
800-947-PLAN

VISA · MasterCard · Discover/Novus

Main	1654 Sq. Ft.
Second	654 Sq. Ft.
Total	2308 Sq. Ft.

© design basics inc.

design basics inc.
HOME PLAN DESIGN SERVICE

LGS1862-23 Manchester

PRICE CODE 23

- ▶ High quality, erasable, reproducible vellums
- ▶ Shipped via 2nd day air within the continental U.S.

- • covered porch and elegant arched windows highlight front elevation
- • 2-story entry showcases stairway and formal dining room with bayed window
- • superb great room has see-thru fireplace and windowed wall for elegant rear view

- • livable island kitchen/breakfast/hearth room features arched window, cathedral ceiling, walk-in pantry and bayed dining
- • second level features interesting sill detail on landing and plant shelf overlooking area below

- • comfortable secondary bedrooms share compartmented bath with separate lavs and clothes chute
- • main level master suite with arched window, volume ceiling, dual lavs, whirlpool tub and two closets

Rear Elevation

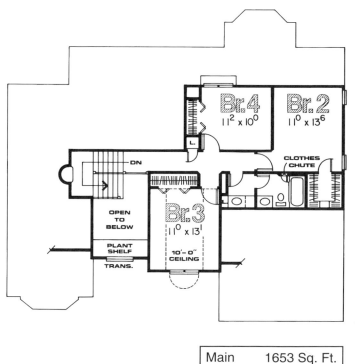

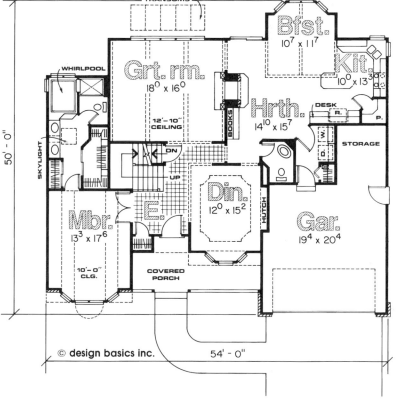

© design basics inc.

Main	1653 Sq. Ft.
Second	700 Sq. Ft.
Total	2353 Sq. Ft.

ORDER DIRECT
7:00-6:00 Mon.-Fri. CST
800-947-PLAN

VISA MasterCard Discover NOVUS

design basics inc.®
HOME PLAN DESIGN SERVICE

49

PRICE CODE

LGS1745-23 Talbot

▶ High quality, erasable, reproducible vellums
▶ Shipped via 2nd day air within the continental U.S.

- wheelchair accessible on main level
- many windows with transoms
- 10-foot ceiling in great room with fireplace, bookcase and wet bar
- gourmet island kitchen with snack bar, pantry and built-in desk
- wrapping windows in dinette allow expansive view to the back
- main level bath/laundry room has window over dryer
- master bedroom with 10-foot ceiling and his and her closets
- luxury master bath features 12-foot ceiling, double vanity and large whirlpool tub
- generous secondary bedrooms
- compartmented bath with sloped ceiling and skylight

Rear Elevation

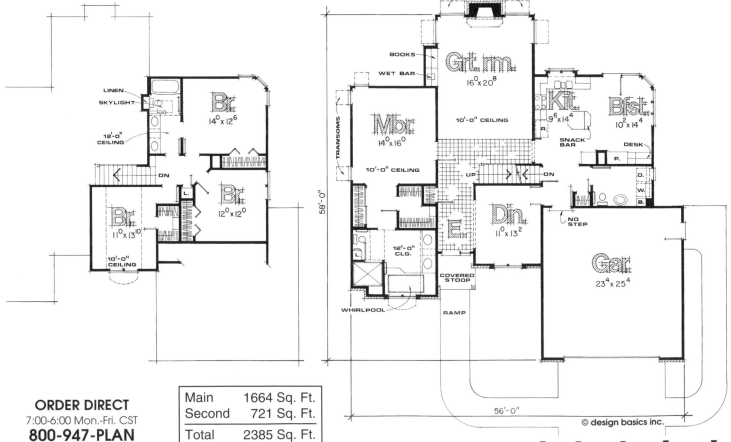

ORDER DIRECT
7:00-6:00 Mon.-Fri. CST

800-947-PLAN

Main	1664 Sq. Ft.
Second	721 Sq. Ft.
Total	2385 Sq. Ft.

© design basics inc.

design basics inc.®
HOME PLAN DESIGN SERVICE

LGS2702-24 Ellison

PRICE CODE

▶ High quality, erasable, reproducible vellums
▶ Shipped via 2nd day air within the continental U.S.

- colonial elevation makes comfortable yet impressive statement
- formal dining room defined by celing treatment and flooring materials
- great room features beautiful windows flanking fireplace

- kitchen features wrap-around counter with lazy Susan, large pantry, handy desk and island
- double doors open to majestic master bedroom with window seat

- pocket door accesses private den from master bedroom
- pampering master bath is accentuated by whirlpool, shower and dual lavs
- secondary bedrooms share convenient compartmented bath

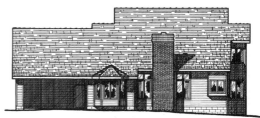

Rear Elevation

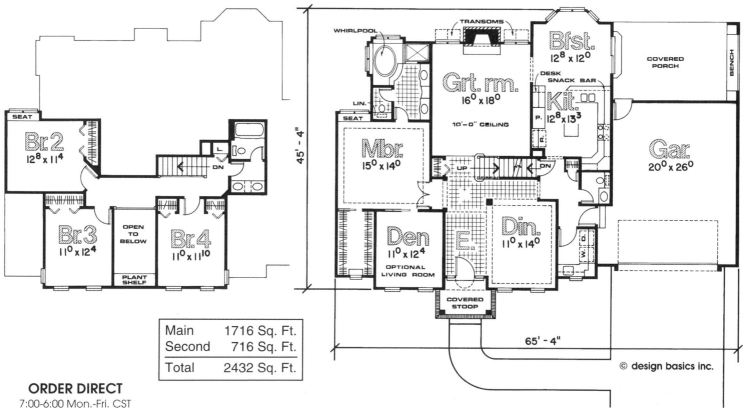

Main	1716 Sq. Ft.
Second	716 Sq. Ft.
Total	2432 Sq. Ft.

© design basics inc.

ORDER DIRECT
7:00-6:00 Mon.-Fri. CST

800-947-PLAN

design basics inc.®
HOME PLAN DESIGN SERVICE

LGS2956-25 Briarwood

PRICE CODE

► High quality, erasable, reproducible vellums
► Shipped via 2nd day air within the continental U.S.

- front porch and arched windows provide a country feel for this attractive elevation
- 15-foot-high arched openings to great room dazzles viewers
- formal dining room easily accessible from large island kitchen

- French doors in breakfast room open to versatile office with sloping 10-foot ceiling
- convenient utility area off kitchen features access to garage, 1/2 bath and generous laundry room complete with folding table

- private entrance into master suite which includes volume ceiling, built-in dresser/linen, two closets and beautiful corner whirlpool with dramatic window treatment
- on second level, 3 large secondary bedrooms share bath with dual lavs

Rear Elevation

Parade Home Package

available for all plans

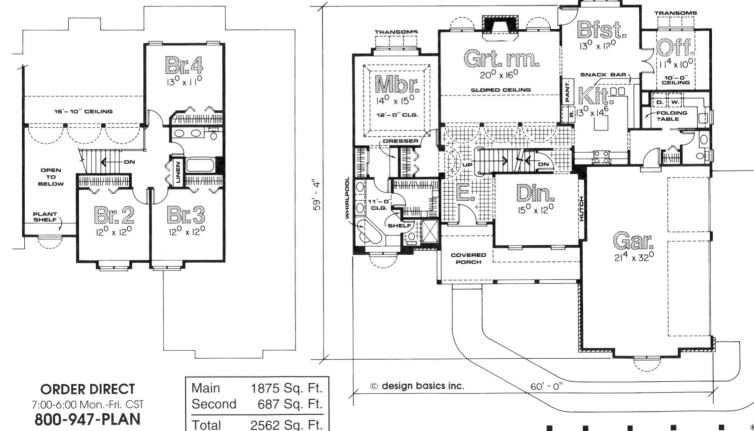

© design basics inc.

60' - 0"

ORDER DIRECT
7:00-6:00 Mon.-Fri. CST
800-947-PLAN

Main	1875 Sq. Ft.
Second	687 Sq. Ft.
Total	2562 Sq. Ft.

52

design basics inc.
HOME PLAN DESIGN SERVICE

LGS2309-25 Edmonton
PRICE CODE

- stone and stucco coupled with excellent lines add intriguing curb appeal
- splendid entry hall surveys formal dining and great rooms with special amenities
- kitchen/breakfast/hearth room features corner walk-in pantry and built-in desk
- great room's see-thru fireplace flanked by pass-thru wet bar/servery and entertainment center
- secondary bedrooms secluded on second level include large closets and share compartmented bath with dual lavs
- French door entry to hall with built-in bookcases between master suite and private den
- exquisite master bath/dressing area with his and her lavs, oval whirlpool and spacious walk-in closet

Rear Elevation

Main	1933 Sq. Ft.
Second	646 Sq. Ft.
Total	2579 Sq. Ft.

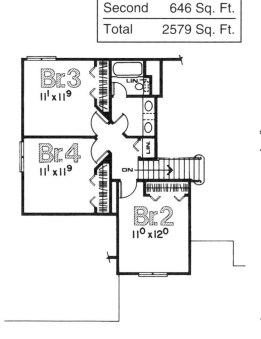

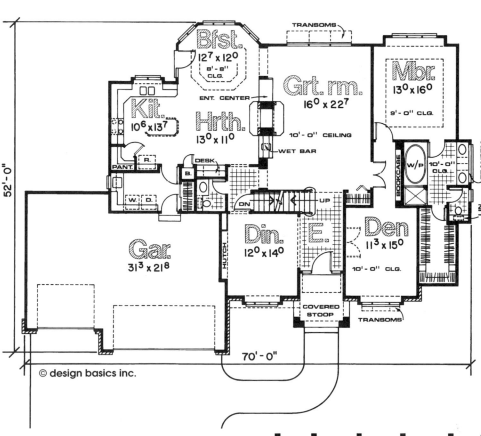

© design basics inc.

design basics inc.
HOME PLAN DESIGN SERVICE

LGS2460-26 Bridgeport

PRICE CODE

Gold Seal
HOME PLANS

- magnificent porch adds appeal to elevation
- volume entry surveys formal living and dining rooms
- formal living room features two bookcases

- impressive great room with three large windows and raised hearth fireplace flanked by bookcases
- captivating gazebo dinette and island kitchen with huge pantry and two lazy Susans

- upstairs, three secondary bedrooms enjoy ample bathroom accommodations and a gallery in the corridor
- main level master suite with porch retreat access, roomy dressing area, his and her vanities and sunlit whirlpool

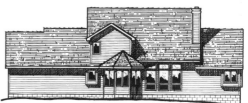

Rear Elevation

Parade Home Package
available for all plans

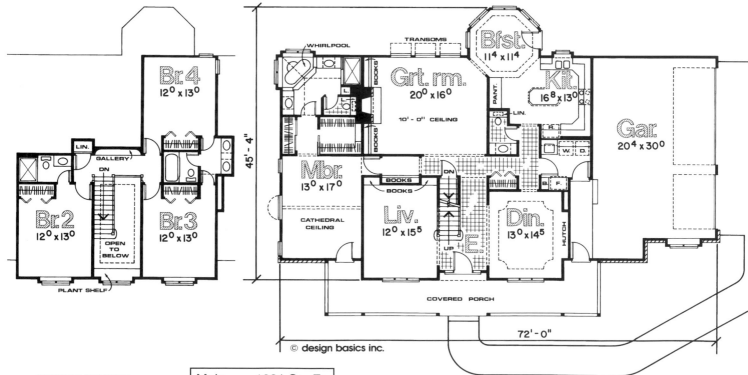

© design basics inc.

Main	1881 Sq. Ft.
Second	814 Sq. Ft.
Total	2695 Sq. Ft.

design basics inc.
HOME PLAN DESIGN SERVICE

LGS2445-28 Kingsbury

PRICE CODE **28**

Gold Seal ™ HOME PLANS

▸ High quality, erasable, reproducible vellums
▸ Shipped via 2nd day air within the continental U.S.

- brick and stucco accents curb appeal
- elegant entry surveys formal living room with volume ceiling and bayed window dining room with hutch space
- window-brightened great room includes see-thru fireplace and built-in bookcases

- gourmet kitchen, bayed dinette and hearth room with see-thru fireplace and bookcase offer enhancements to family living
- boxed ceiling and arched-opening view highlight second floor corridor

- secondary bedrooms enjoy compartmented bath with dual lavs and huge linen cabinet
- secluded main floor master suite features tiered ceiling, walk-in closet, luxury bath with whirlpool and his and her vanities

Rear Elevation

Unfinished Storage Adds 261 Square Feet

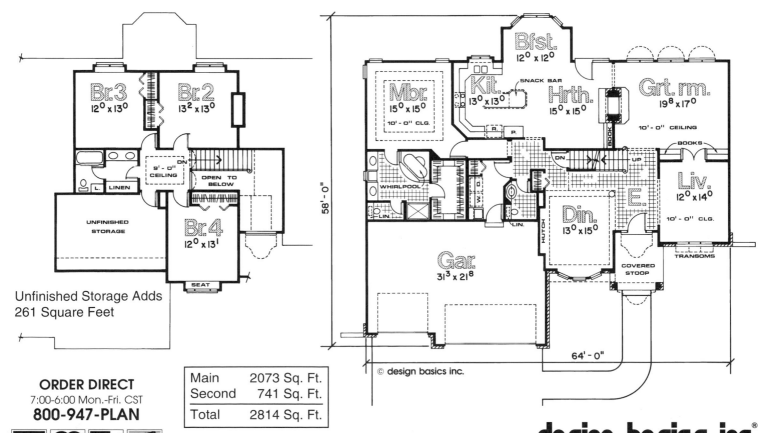

© design basics inc.

ORDER DIRECT
7:00-6:00 Mon.-Fri. CST
800-947-PLAN

Main	2073 Sq. Ft.	
Second	741 Sq. Ft.	
Total	2814 Sq. Ft.	

VISA MasterCard AMERICAN EXPRESS DISCOVER NOVUS Cards

design basics inc. ®
HOME PLAN DESIGN SERVICE

LGS2671-30 Durand

PRICE CODE

- ▶ High quality, erasable, reproducible vellums
- ▶ Shipped via 2nd day air within the continental U.S.

- • fluted columns and decorative mouldings at the grand entrance present a stately, dignified exterior
- • formal dining room and parlor open to volume entry with graceful flared staircase

- • comfortable great room with boxed-beam ceiling and raised-hearth fireplace brightened by arched transom windows
- • strategically located wet bar serves the dining room and the great room

- • luxurious master suite enjoys privacy with secluded entrance
- • viewed from entry, French doors open to spacious upper-level media room complete with entertainment center and 2 built-in desks

Rear Elevation

Parade Home Package

available for all plans

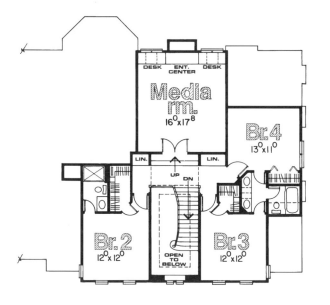

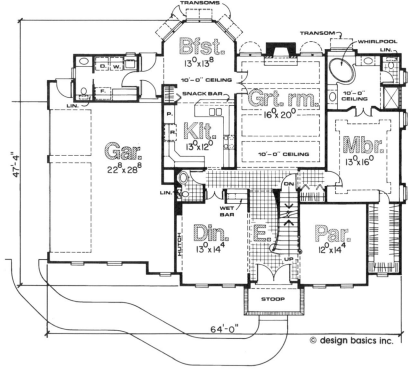

© design basics inc.

Main	1923 Sq. Ft.
Lower	1106 Sq. Ft.
Total	3029 Sq. Ft.

ORDER DIRECT
7:00-6:00 Mon.-Fri. CST
800-947-PLAN

design basics inc.
HOME PLAN DESIGN SERVICE

TWO
STORY
HOMES

LGS2579-15 Bartels

PRICE CODE

▶ High quality, erasable, reproducible vellums
▶ Shipped via 2nd day air within the continental U.S.

Gold Seal HOME PLANS™

- columned front porch adds visual appeal to this livable design
- from the entry, step down into living room distinguished by raised hearth fireplace centered under cathedral ceiling
- French doors seclude formal dining room from kitchen
- ample kitchen and dinette provide amenities available in larger plans such as large pantry and center island with snack bar
- private den strategically located off dinette
- grand master bath features dual lavs and whirlpool
- spacious walk-in closet highlights master bedroom

G. MacDonald

Rear Elevation

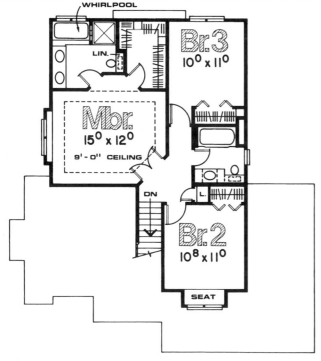

WHIRLPOOL

LIN.

Br.3
10⁰ x 11⁰

Mbr.
15⁰ x 12⁰
9'-0" CEILING

DN

Br.2
10⁸ x 11⁰

SEAT

L.

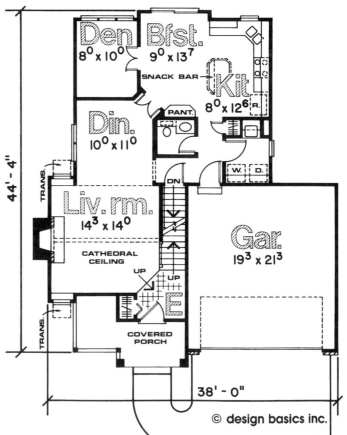

Den
8⁰ x 10⁰

Bfst.
9⁰ x 13⁷

SNACK BAR

Kit.
8⁰ x 12⁶

PANT.

Din.
10⁰ x 11⁰

W. D.

TRANS.

Liv. rm.
14³ x 14⁰

DN

CATHEDRAL CEILING

UP

UP

Gar.
19³ x 21³

TRANS.

COVERED PORCH

44' - 4"

38' - 0"

© design basics inc.

ORDER DIRECT

7:00-6:00 Mon.-Fri. CST

800-947-PLAN

Main	869 SQ. FT.
Second	725 SQ. FT.
Total	1594 SQ. FT.

58

design basics inc.®
HOME PLAN DESIGN SERVICE

LGS3098-16 Duncan

PRICE CODE

▸ High quality, erasable, reproducible vellums
▸ Shipped via 2nd day air within the continental U.S.

- 2-story entry with plant shelf, open to great room
- formal dining and great room are well arranged for entertaining

- breakfast area features large patio door and useful built-in bookcase
- kitchen has 2 lazy Susans and snack bar
- upstairs, secondary bedrooms have ample closet space and hall bath

- bedroom #2 offers a built-in desk
- terrific master suite offers his and her closets and compartmented whirlpool bath

Rear Elevation

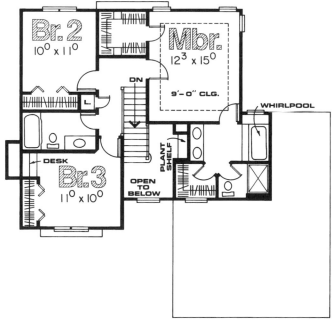

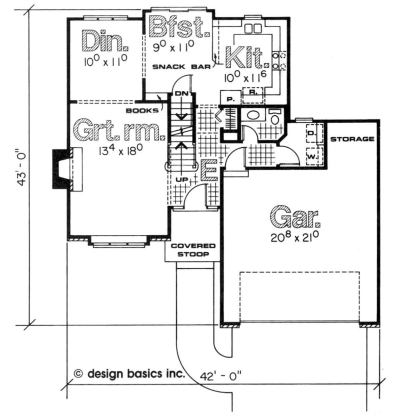

© design basics inc.

42' - 0"

43' - 0"

ORDER DIRECT
7:00-6:00 Mon.-Fri. CST
800-947-PLAN

Main	831 Sq. Ft.
Second	790 Sq. Ft.
Total	1621 Sq. Ft.

design basics inc.
HOME PLAN DESIGN SERVICE

LGS2248-16 Laverton

PRICE CODE

Gold Seal™ HOME PLANS

- quaint covered porch
- volume entry with decorator plant ledge above closet
- formal dining room with boxed window seen from entry

- large great room with fireplace and boxed window out the back
- open dinette with built-in desk
- pantry and window above sink in kitchen
- window and closet in laundry room
- upstairs landing overlooks entry below

- bedroom #3 with beautiful arched window under volume ceiling
- master bedroom with walk-in closet and pampering dressing area with double vanity and whirlpool under window

Rear Elevation

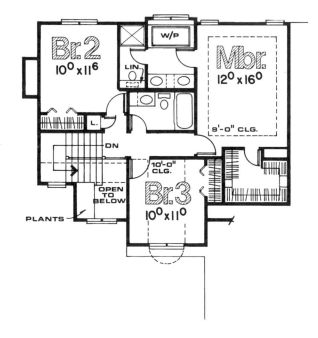

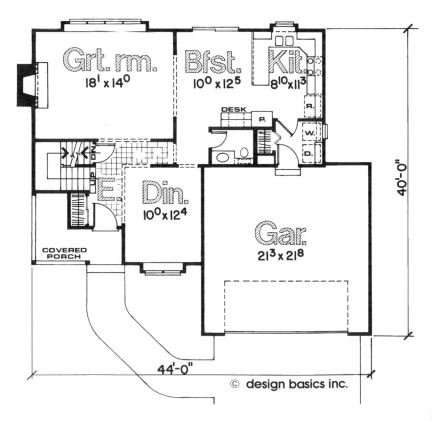

© design basics inc.

Main	891	SQ. FT.
Second	759	SQ. FT.
Total	1650	SQ. FT.

design basics inc.
HOME PLAN DESIGN SERVICE

LGS2545-17 Deming

PRICE CODE

▸ **High quality, erasable, reproducible vellums**
▸ **Shipped via 2nd day air within the continental U.S.**

Gold Seal
HOME PLANS

- quaint covered porch suggests comfortable living in this two-story design
- great room features raised hearth fireplace, sloped ceiling and transom windows that allow more natural light
- wrap-around kitchen with peninsula snack bar is located between formal dining room and family dinette
- staircase with nostalgic wood railing offers dramatic view of great room
- double doors invite you into master bedroom with high 10-foot ceiling
- master bath with dual lavs, whirlpool and shower adjoins large closet
- large linen closet services upstairs bath areas

Rear Elevation

Parade Home Package
available for all plans

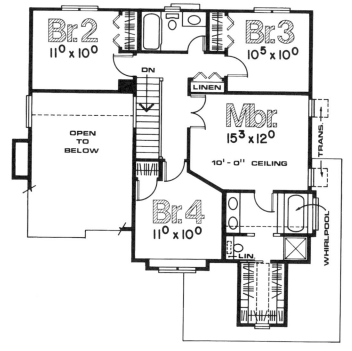

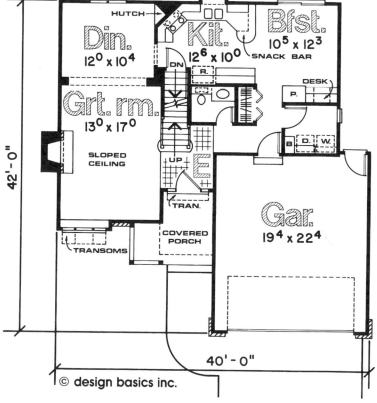

ORDER DIRECT
7:00-6:00 Mon.-Fri. CST
800-947-PLAN

VISA MasterCard DISCOVER NOVUS

Main	845 SQ. FT.
Second	883 SQ. FT.
Total	1728 SQ. FT.

© design basics inc.

61

design basics inc.
HOME PLAN DESIGN SERVICE

LGS3097-PRICE CODE **17** Lincoln

▶ High quality, erasable, reproducible vellums
▶ Shipped via 2nd day air within the continental U.S.

- traditional elevation combines aesthetics and economy
- symmetrical coat closets and cased openings frame view to great room and entry
- versatile dining room has parlor option

- bayed dinette with back yard access and staircase to second level
- deluxe laundry room and built-in bookcase provide ample amenities to fantastic upper level

- luxurious master suite contains built-in dresser between his and her walk-in closets
- roomy compartmented dressing area with whirlpool
- extra storage in deep garage

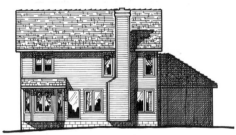

Rear Elevation

PROMOTIONAL LICENSE • Black and White, Camera-Ready Artwork of the home plan FREE with any plan purchase to assist you in advertising the home.

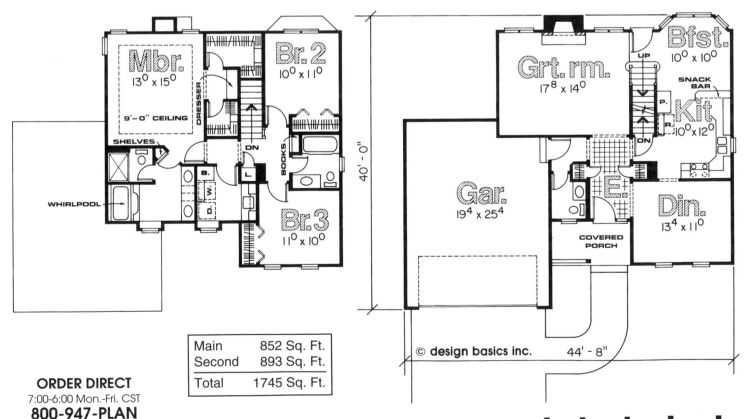

Main	852 Sq. Ft.
Second	893 Sq. Ft.
Total	1745 Sq. Ft.

ORDER DIRECT
7:00-6:00 Mon.-Fri. CST
800-947-PLAN

design basics inc.®
HOME PLAN DESIGN SERVICE

LGS3581-17 Paige

PRICE CODE

▶ High quality, erasable, reproducible vellums
▶ Shipped via 2nd day air within the continental U.S.

- quaint, cozy exterior
- covered porch leads to entry with double-door coat closet
- formal dining room is flexible as parlor
- sunny kitchen has wrapping counters

- patio doors leads to back from breakfast area
- spacious family room boasts fireplace and three lovely windows
- extra deep garage offers storage options

- second floor master suite hosts roomy walk-in closet and whirlpool tub
- three secondary bedrooms share central hall bath
- open area above entry easily converts to optional toy closet

Rear Elevation

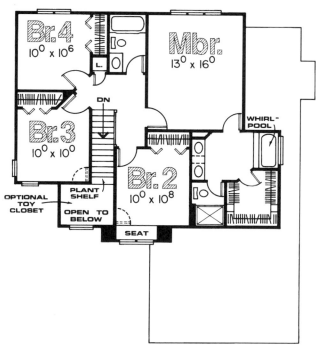

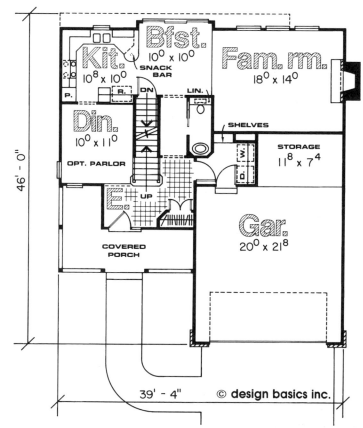

Main	866 Sq. Ft.
Second	905 Sq. Ft.
Total	1771 Sq. Ft.

© design basics inc.

design basics inc.®
HOME PLAN DESIGN SERVICE

LGS2308-17 Juniper

PRICE CODE **17**

Gold Seal HOME PLANS™

▶ High quality, erasable, reproducible vellums
▶ Shipped via 2nd day air within the continental U.S.

- sleek lines, covered porch and window details enhance elevation
- volume entry views bright living room with adjoining dining room
- kitchen enjoys gourmet features and bayed dinette

- family room enhanced by window-brightened wall and raised-hearth fireplace
- garage includes extra storage space
- bedroom #2 includes huge walk-in closet
- secondary bedrooms convenient to bath

- hall design affords seclusion to luxurious master suite with boxed ceiling
- pampering master bath/dressing area includes two closets, whirlpool with plant sill and double lavs

Rear Elevation

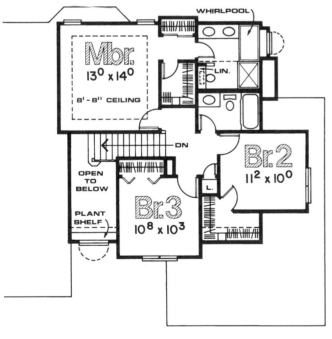

© design basics inc.

Main	1032 Sq. Ft.
Second	743 Sq. Ft.
Total	1775 Sq. Ft.

64

design basics inc®
HOME PLAN DESIGN SERVICE

LGS2699-18 Benson

PRICE CODE

- brick and glass block accents, plus wood-railed porch create front elevation that's contemporary, yet nostalgic
- dining room offers ample space for formal dinner occasions
- family room with raised hearth fireplace provides open feeling and endless decorating options
- kitchen features 2 lazy Susans, centrally-placed range and handy snack bar
- master bath is conveniently laid out with separate vanities
- master bedroom boasts 9-foot-high ceiling and spacious dressing area
- well-appointed master bath includes step-up whirlpool and plant shelf

Rear Elevation

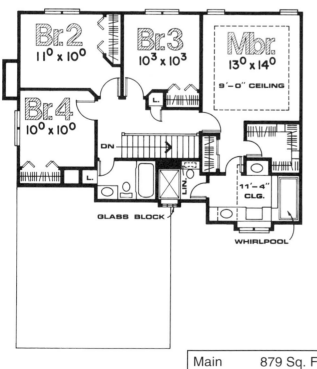

Br. 2
11⁰ x 10⁰

Br. 3
10³ x 10³

Mbr.
13⁰ x 14⁰
9'-0" CEILING

Br. 4
10⁰ x 10⁰

DN

11'-4" CLG.

GLASS BLOCK

WHIRLPOOL

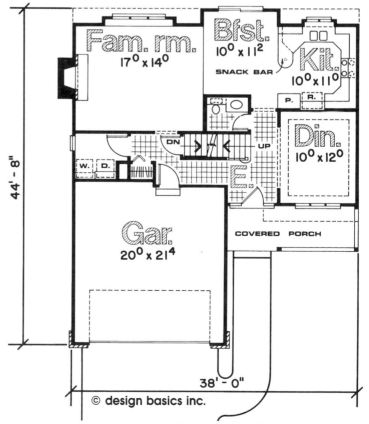

Fam. rm.
17⁰ x 14⁰

Bfst.
10⁰ x 11²
SNACK BAR

Kit.
10⁰ x 11⁰

P. R.

DN UP

Din.
10⁰ x 12⁰

W. D.

Gar.
20⁰ x 21⁴

COVERED PORCH

44'-8"

38'-0"

© design basics inc.

Main	879 Sq. Ft.
Second	945 Sq. Ft.
Total	1824 Sq. Ft.

design basics inc.®
HOME PLAN DESIGN SERVICE

65

LGS1868-**18** Somerset

PRICE CODE

- appealing porch graces elevation
- light and airy 2-story entrance with large guest closet and plant shelf above
- formal dining room encourages intimate meals or entertaining options
- row of picture/awning windows showcase great room with striking fireplace
- expansive island kitchen and bayed breakfast area with open view to back yard
- secondary bedrooms afford comfort and privacy
- lovely master suite with tiered ceiling includes compartmented bath, two walk-in closets, dual lavs and whirlpool tub

Rear Elevation

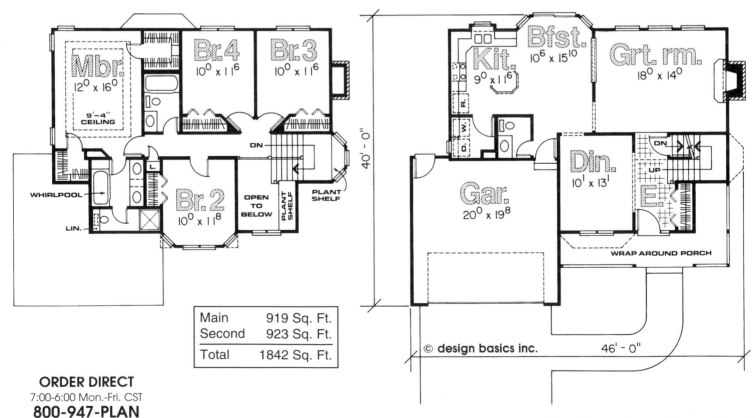

Mbr. 12⁰ x 16⁰
9'-4" CEILING
Br.4 10⁰ x 11⁶
Br.3 10⁰ x 11⁶
DN
WHIRLPOOL
LIN.
Br. 2 10⁰ x 11⁸
OPEN TO BELOW
PLANT SHELF
PLANT SHELF

Kit. 9⁰ x 11⁶
Bfst. 10⁶ x 15¹⁰
Grt. rm. 18⁰ x 14⁰
D. W. R.
Gar. 20⁰ x 19⁸
Din. 10¹ x 13¹
DN
UP
WRAP AROUND PORCH

40' - 0"

46' - 0"

© design basics inc.

Main	919 Sq. Ft.
Second	923 Sq. Ft.
Total	1842 Sq. Ft.

ORDER DIRECT
7:00-6:00 Mon.-Fri. CST
800-947-PLAN

66

design basics inc.
HOME PLAN DESIGN SERVICE

LGS2235-19 Albany

PRICE CODE

Gold Seal™
HOME PLANS

- inviting covered porch
- interesting staircase with landing in volume entry
- abundant windows throughout
- 10-foot ceiling and handsome fireplace in great room

- island counter, pantry and desk in open kitchen/dinette area
- kitchen conveniently accesses laundry room
- upstairs landing overlooks entry below

- beautiful arched window under volume ceiling in bedroom #2
- master suite features pampering dressing area with double vanity, compartmented stool and shower plus whirlpool under window

Rear Elevation

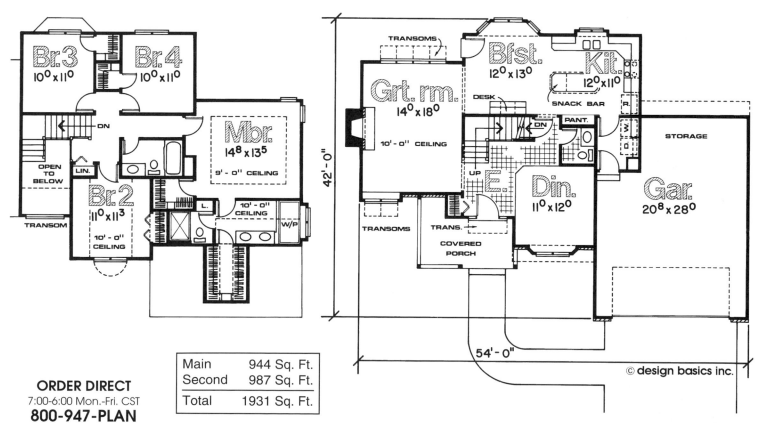

© design basics inc.

Main	944 Sq. Ft.
Second	987 Sq. Ft.
Total	1931 Sq. Ft.

design basics inc.®
HOME PLAN DESIGN SERVICE

LGS2648-19 Cyprus

PRICE CODE 19

Gold Seal™ HOME PLANS

▶ High quality, erasable, reproducible vellums
▶ Shipped via 2nd day air within the continental U.S.

- brilliant design character captures great livability in this striking 2-story home
- whether used as office, library, or as formal living room, parlor with privacy is valuable design

- T-shaped staircase smooths traffic flow
- well-appointed kitchen is just steps away from dinette and dining room
- integrated design of family room, dinette and kitchen capitalize on comfortable family living and easy entertaining

- charming window seat complements comfortable master bedroom
- all desired amenities such as walk-in closet, dual lavs and whirlpool are featured in master bath

Rear Elevation

Parade Home Package
available for all plans

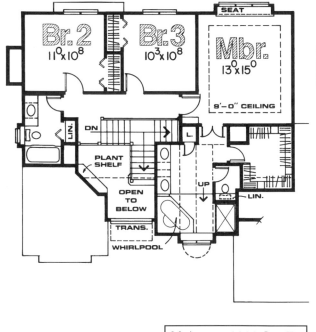

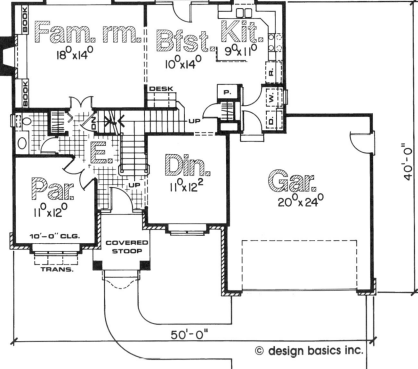

Main	1082 Sq. Ft.
Second	869 Sq. Ft.
Total	**1951 Sq. Ft.**

ORDER DIRECT
7:00-6:00 Mon.-Fri. CST
800-947-PLAN

© design basics inc.

design basics inc.®
HOME PLAN DESIGN SERVICE

LGS2315-**19** Harrisburg

▶ High quality, erasable, reproducible vellums
▶ Shipped via 2nd day air within the continental U.S.

- stately front elevation gives dynamic impact
- dramatic French doors connect formal living room and family room
- family room enhanced by raised hearth fireplace and bayed conversation area

- gourmet kitchen/breakfast area profits from extra-large pantry, two lazy Susans and patio door to the rear yard
- attractive stairway leads to second floor corridor with bookcase and large linen closet

- arrangement of secondary bedrooms gives privacy but remain within easy access to a roomy bath
- master suite enjoys volume ceiling, built-in bookcase and luxurious compartmented bath/dressing area

Rear Elevation

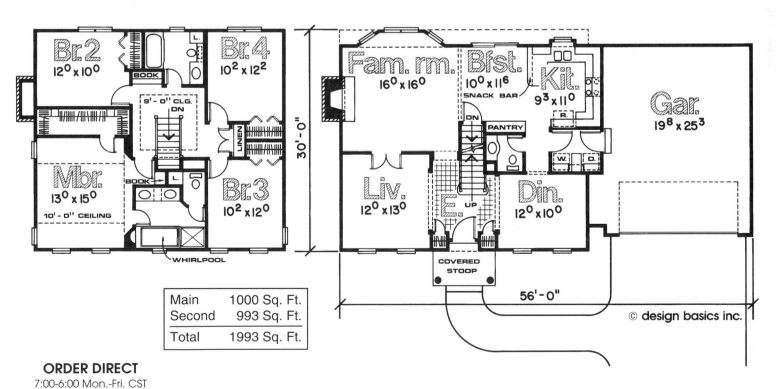

Main	1000 Sq. Ft.
Second	993 Sq. Ft.
Total	1993 Sq. Ft.

© design basics inc.

ORDER DIRECT
7:00-6:00 Mon.-Fri. CST
800-947-PLAN

design basics inc®
HOME PLAN DESIGN SERVICE

LGS1870-20 Bristol

PRICE CODE **20**

Gold Seal
HOME PLANS™

- charming porch and arched windows of elevation allude to elegance within
- parlor with large bayed window and sloped ceiling harks back to simpler life
- formal dining area open to parlor invites entertaining with ease from kitchen

- bright kitchen and bayed breakfast area features wrapping counters, pantry and desk
- step down into expansive gathering room with fireplace and abundant windows

- ample secondary bedrooms share nearby skylit bath
- indulging master bedroom with skylit dressing area, dual lavs, whirlpool tub and large walk-in closet

Rear Elevation

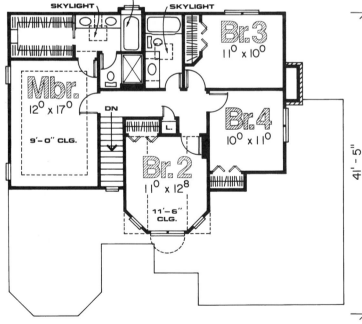

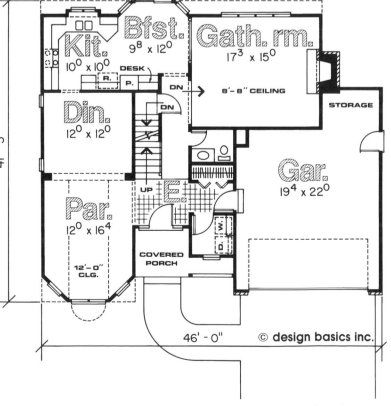

© design basics inc.

Main	1113 Sq. Ft.
Second	965 Sq. Ft.
Total	2078 Sq. Ft.

ORDER DIRECT
7:00-6:00 Mon.-Fri. CST
800-947-PLAN

70

design basics inc.®
HOME PLAN DESIGN SERVICE

LGS2618-21 Paisley

PRICE CODE

▶ **High quality, erasable, reproducible vellums**
▶ **Shipped via 2nd day air within the continental U.S.**

- beautifully proportioned design is complemented by large covered porch framed with wood railing
- living room is enhanced by warmth of a bayed window and double French doors opening to family room
- spacious dining room is accented by built-in curio cabinet
- efficient kitchen is just steps away from dinette and dining room
- family room is perfect for informal gatherings
- laundry room is conveniently accessible from kitchen, garage and directly outside
- storage space abounds in garage area
- double doors open to luxurious master bedroom with distinctive vaulted ceiling

Rear Elevation

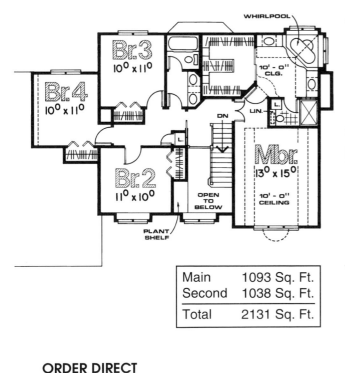

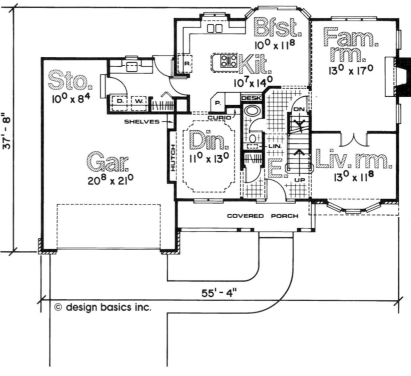

Main	1093 SQ. FT.
Second	1038 SQ. FT.
Total	2131 SQ. FT.

© design basics inc.

ORDER DIRECT
7:00-6:00 Mon.-Fri. CST
800-947-PLAN

71

LGS2216-21 Collier

PRICE CODE

▶ **High quality, erasable, reproducible vellums**
▶ **Shipped via 2nd day air within the continental U.S.**

- inviting covered porch
- entry open to formal living room with volume ceiling
- abundant windows throughout
- dining room open to living room for versatility

- step down into comfortable family room with fireplace
- den with bookcase can easily open up to family room with French doors if desired
- pantry and desk in kitchen open to bayed dinette

- upstairs, bedroom #2 offers volume ceiling and half-round window
- skylit hall bath
- private master suite features plant shelf, whirlpool, skylight above vanity and walk-in closet

Rear Elevation

S. JANICEK

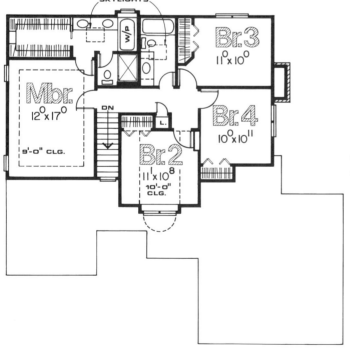

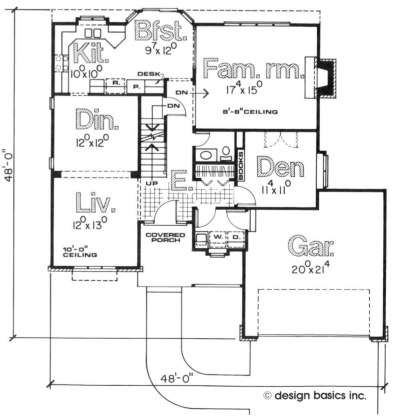

48'-0"

48'-0"

© design basics inc.

ORDER DIRECT
7:00-6:00 Mon.-Fri. CST
800-947-PLAN

Main	1224 Sq. Ft.
Second	950 Sq. Ft.
Total	2174 Sq. Ft.

design basics inc.
HOME PLAN DESIGN SERVICE

LGS3588-21 Stratman

PRICE CODE

▶ High quality, erasable, reproducible vellums
▶ Shipped via 2nd day air within the continental U.S.

- notable windows offer insight into home
- living room decorated with arched window and volume ceiling
- dining room leads to kitchen through French doors

- wet bar, fireplace and beautiful windows in casual family room
- bayed breakfast area accesses back
- kitchen includes island counter and two lazy Susans

- soaking sink in laundry room
- master suite has 9'-0" ceiling, skylight and whirlpool tub with separate shower
- room for expansion on second floor

Rear Elevation

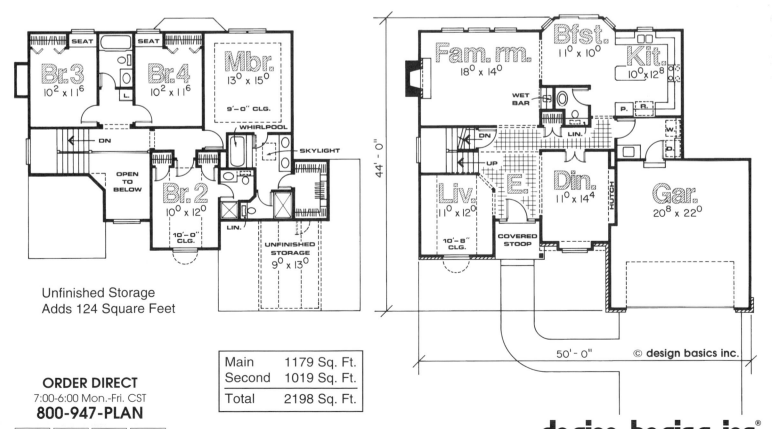

Unfinished Storage
Adds 124 Square Feet

ORDER DIRECT
7:00-6:00 Mon.-Fri. CST
800-947-PLAN

Main	1179 Sq. Ft.
Second	1019 Sq. Ft.
Total	2198 Sq. Ft.

design basics inc.
HOME PLAN DESIGN SERVICE

LGS1019-22 Hazelton

PRICE CODE

Gold Seal™
HOME PLANS

- open central core at staircase
- 10-foot ceiling in great room with fireplace as focal point
- large, beautiful boxed windows at front and back of great room
- formal, tiered ceiling in dining room

- large island kitchen and dinette
- laundry room with coat closet serves as mud entry from garage
- additional storage space in garage
- secondary bedrooms share central bath with double vanity

- master bedroom at top of stairs buffered from secondary bedrooms
- master bath area includes double lav vanity, whirlpool tub, large walk-in closet and skylight

Rear Elevation

ORIGINAL DRAFT
ALL DESIGN BASICS PLANS HAVE BEEN REGISTERED WITH THE U.S. COPYRIGHT OFFICE

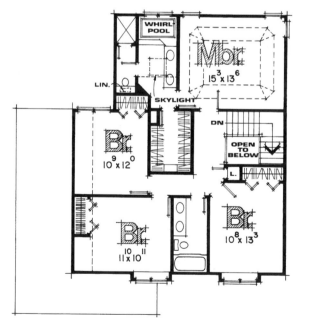

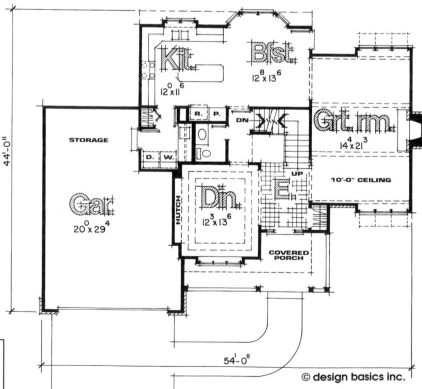

Main	1132	Sq. Ft.
Second	1087	Sq. Ft.
Total	2219	Sq. Ft.

© design basics inc.

ORDER DIRECT
7:00-6:00 Mon.-Fri. CST

800-947-PLAN

design basics inc.®
HOME PLAN DESIGN SERVICE

LGS3333-23 Hartman

PRICE CODE 23

► High quality, erasable, reproducible vellums
► Shipped via 2nd day air within the continental U.S.

- cozy front porch enhances elevation packed with windows
- stacked living and dining rooms combine giving flexibility to formal entertaining
- well-organized kitchen is open to bayed breakfast area with back yard access

- huge family room with fireplace is great for relaxing family times
- private den is located off the entry through French doors
- master suite with vaulted 9-foot ceiling is complimented by large walk-in closet

- pampering master bath boasts luxurious sunlit whirlpool tub with separate shower and twin vanities
- three secondary bedrooms share large, centralized, compartmented bath

Rear Elevation

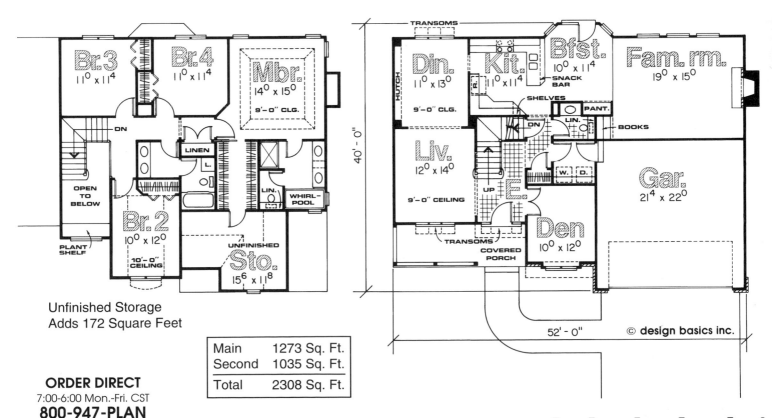

Unfinished Storage
Adds 172 Square Feet

Main	1273 Sq. Ft.
Second	1035 Sq. Ft.
Total	2308 Sq. Ft.

© design basics inc.

design basics inc.
HOME PLAN DESIGN SERVICE

LGS2962-23 Baldwin

PRICE CODE 23

Gold Seal™ HOME PLANS

- country charm is achieved with a front porch and well-proportioned gables
- functional T-stairs add flair to entry
- media room off bayed family room offers great versatility for formal and informal gatherings

- bayed breakfast area with back yard access is open to efficient island kitchen with corner pantry
- bonus storage space in garage
- upstairs, 3 secondary bedrooms share a terrific compartmented bath

- elegant balcony overlooking 2-story entry reveals secluded entrance into master suite via French doors
- master suite has walk-in closet and spacious whirlpool bath with open shower

Rear Elevation

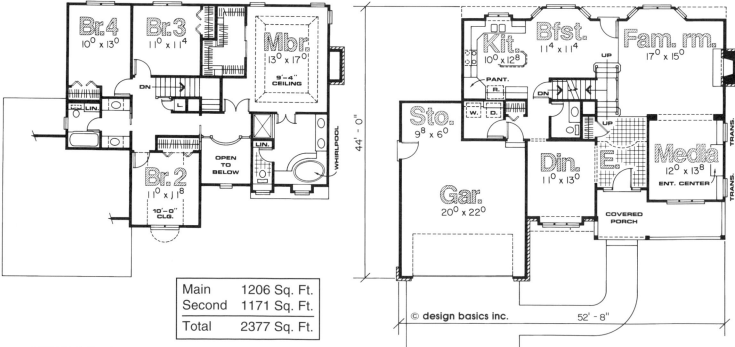

Main	1206 Sq. Ft.
Second	1171 Sq. Ft.
Total	2377 Sq. Ft.

© design basics inc.

design basics inc.®
HOME PLAN DESIGN SERVICE

LGS1553-23 Kendall

PRICE CODE **23**

▶ High quality, erasable, reproducible vellums
▶ Shipped via 2nd day air within the continental U.S.

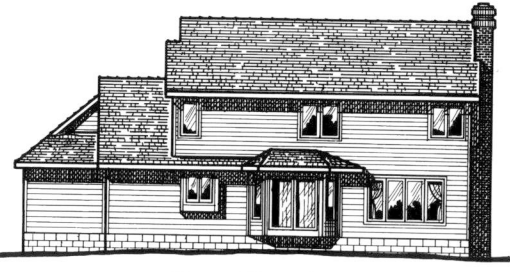

Gold Seal™ HOME PLANS

- bright 2-story entry with plant shelf
- hard surface trafficways
- central hall formalizes front half of the house
- French doors connect family room and living room with enticing bayed window

- efficient kitchen with snack bar and pantry is open to bayed breakfast area with planning desk
- salad sink and counter space doubles as servery for formal dining room

- master bedroom offers volume ceiling and arched window
- master bath features walk-through closet/transition area and corner whirlpool
- interesting angles add design character to bedrooms

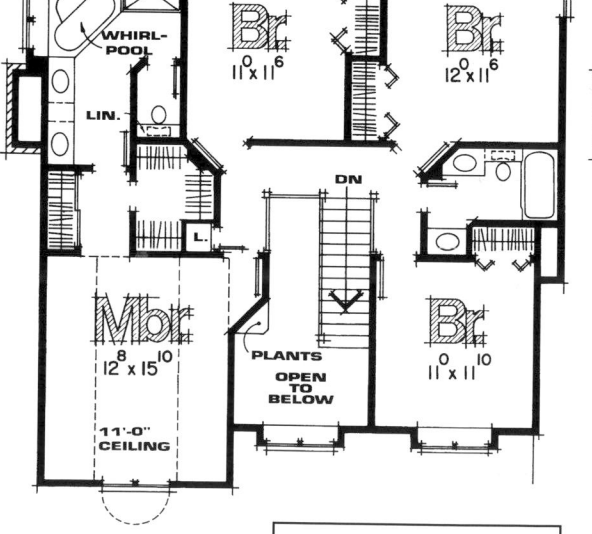

Rear Elevation

Main	1303 Sq. Ft.
Second	1084 Sq. Ft.
Total	2387 Sq. Ft.

© design basics inc.

ORDER DIRECT

7:00-6:00 Mon.-Fri. CST

800-947-PLAN

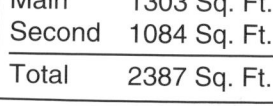

design basics inc.®
HOME PLAN DESIGN SERVICE

LGS2949-24 Hartley

PRICE CODE

Gold Seal — HOME PLANS

- ▶ **High quality, erasable, reproducible vellums**
- ▶ **Shipped via 2nd day air within the continental U.S.**

- gabled roof and simple foundation provides affordability to this wonderful 2-story
- generous stairway landing overlooks 2-story great room highlighted by built-in cabinets surrounding a tile fireplace

- formal dining room features built-in wet bar/buffet
- well-integrated kitchen and breakfast area offers island sink with snack bar
- upstairs 3 secondary bedrooms share compartmented bath with two lavs

- cathedral ceiling with arched transom at 11-foot-high brings sophistication to master bedroom
- angled whirlpool tub, his and her vanities, walk-in closet and private shower highlight master bath

Rear Elevation

Parade Home Package

available for all plans

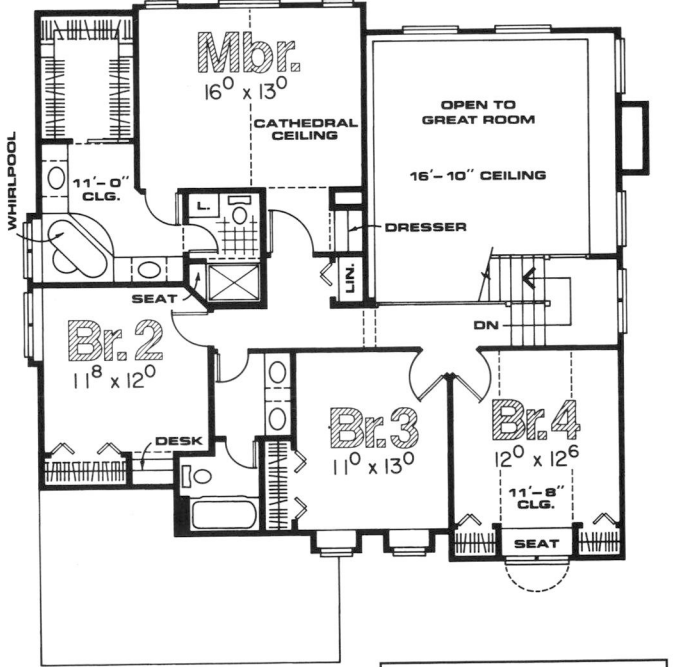

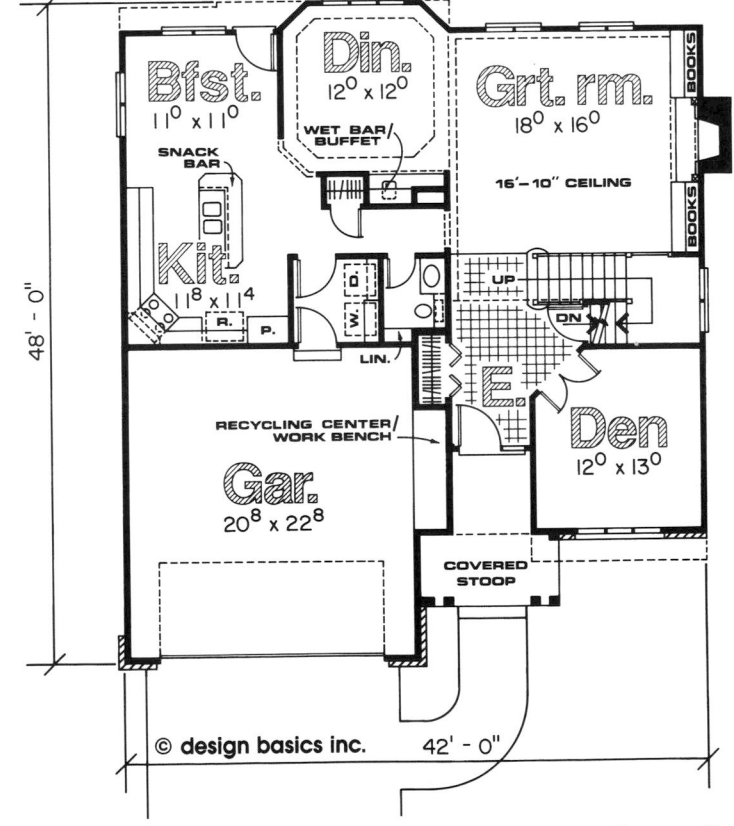

Main	1216 Sq. Ft.
Second	1188 Sq. Ft.
Total	2404 Sq. Ft.

ORDER DIRECT
7:00-6:00 Mon.-Fri. CST
800-947-PLAN

design basics inc.
HOME PLAN DESIGN SERVICE

LGS3377-25 Chilton

PRICE CODE

- gabled windows combine with intricate front porch to create sense of welcome
- see-thru fireplace and 11'-0" ceiling illuminate living room
- family room displays three arched windows and 11'-0" ceiling
- T-shaped staircase has attractive wood railing and landing overlooking family room
- breakfast area reveals planning desk and boxed window
- kitchen equipped with snack bar and sun-lit sink area
- vaulted ceiling and oval whirlpool accentuate private master suite
- master suite closet can easily be expanded
- large closet convenient off laundry room with soaking sink
- 9'-0" main level walls

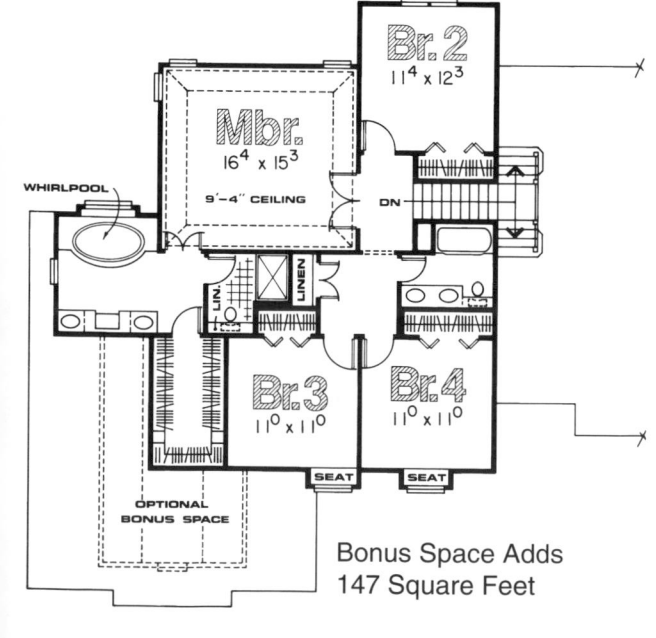

Rear Elevation

Bonus Space Adds
147 Square Feet

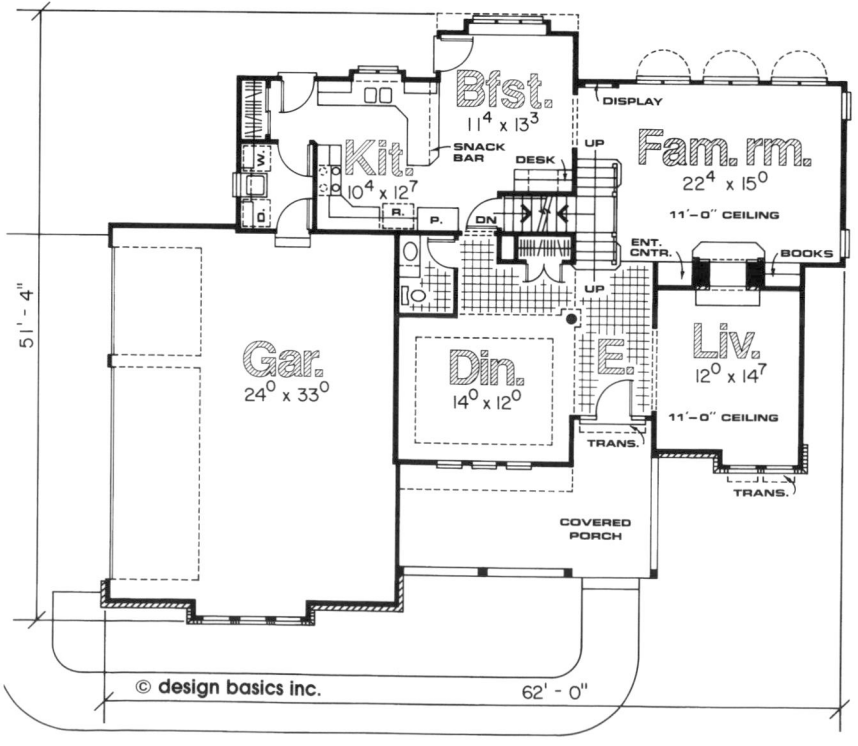

© design basics inc.

ORDER DIRECT
7:00-6:00 Mon.-Fri. CST
800-947-PLAN

Main	1406 Sq. Ft.
Second	1137 Sq. Ft.
Total	2543 Sq. Ft.

design basics inc.
HOME PLAN DESIGN SERVICE

LGS1455-PRICE CODE **25** Newberry

▶ **High quality, erasable, reproducible vellums**
▶ **Shipped via 2nd day air within the continental U.S.**

- dreamy wrap-around porch
- French doors between living room and dining room
- island kitchen with snack bar, pantry and lazy Susan

- planning desk in dinette adjoining sunroom
- sunken family room with beamed ceiling and fireplace located in back for multiple furniture arrangements
- vaulted ceiling in master bedroom
- extra wide hallway with linen closet

- French doors into spacious master bath with dramatic bayed window at corner whirlpool tub
- secondary bedrooms share compartmented hall bath with 2 vanities
- optional play area in third bedroom

Rear Elevation

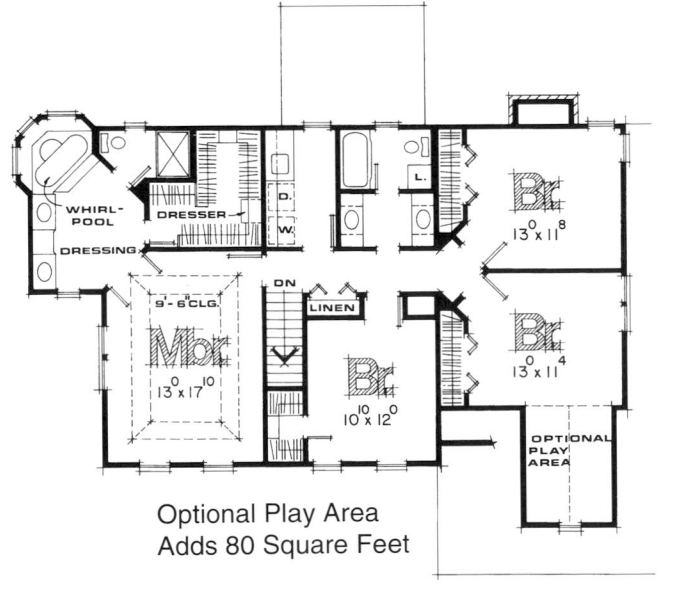

Optional Play Area
Adds 80 Square Feet

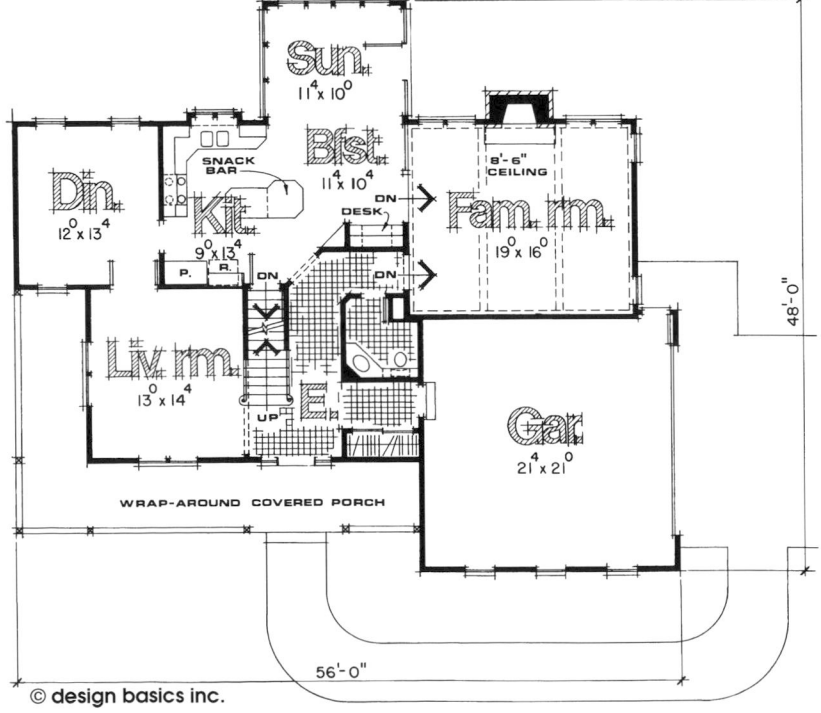

© design basics inc.

Main	1322 Sq. Ft.
Second	1272 Sq. Ft.
Total	2594 Sq. Ft.

ORDER DIRECT
7:00-6:00 Mon.-Fri. CST
800-947-PLAN

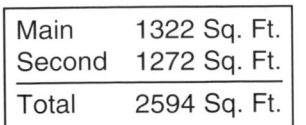

80

LGS2779-26 Leawood

PRICE CODE **26**

- handsome rooflines balance with brick and siding to provide appeal to front elevation
- double doors open to den featuring tall windows and spider-beamed ceiling
- open family room features fireplace and large built-in media center
- bayed dinette has exit to outdoors
- kitchen features island cooktop, large pantry and desk
- angled double doors open to secluded master bedroom with boxed ceiling and huge walk-in closet
- master bathroom contains dual lavs and glass block over step-up whirlpool
- secondary bedrooms are well removed from master suite

Gold Seal HOME PLANS™

Rear Elevation

Br. 3 12⁰ x 12⁰

Br. 2 12⁰ x 12⁰

Br. 4 11⁰ x 13⁰ 10'-0" CEILING

LIN. GLASS BLOCK WHIRLPOOL

DRESSING SEAT

Mbr. 14⁰ x 18⁰ 9'-0" CEILING

DN OPEN TO BELOW TRANSOM

D.W. **Kit.** 11⁶ x 13⁰ B. P. R.

Bfst. 11⁰ x 15⁰ DESK

Fam. rm. 16⁰ x 18⁰ ENT. CENTER

WET BAR

Gar. 22⁸ x 34⁰

HUTCH DN UP

Din. 12⁰ x 15⁰

Den 12⁸ x 14⁷ 11'-0" CLG.

TRANS. COVERED STOOP TRANSOMS

50'-0"

56'-0"

© design basics inc.

Main	1415 Sq. Ft.
Second	1274 Sq. Ft.
Total	2689 Sq. Ft.

design basics inc.®
HOME PLAN DESIGN SERVICE

82

LGS3246-26 Jennings

PRICE CODE **26**

- decorative windows and expansive covered porch highlight this 2-story home
- formal dining room offers hutch space and access to kitchen/breakfast area
- French doors in formal living room open to spacious family room
- bayed windows, entertainment center and see-thru fireplace compliment family room
- large breakfast area with bookcase is warmed by fireplace
- gourmet kitchen has island cooktop, pantry and lazy Susan
- boxed ceiling and large his and her walk-in closets accentuate master bedroom
- French doors reveal master bath with ceiling accents, skylight and whirlpool
- spacious secondary bedrooms share compartmented hall bath

Rear Elevation

ALL PLANS *Customizable*

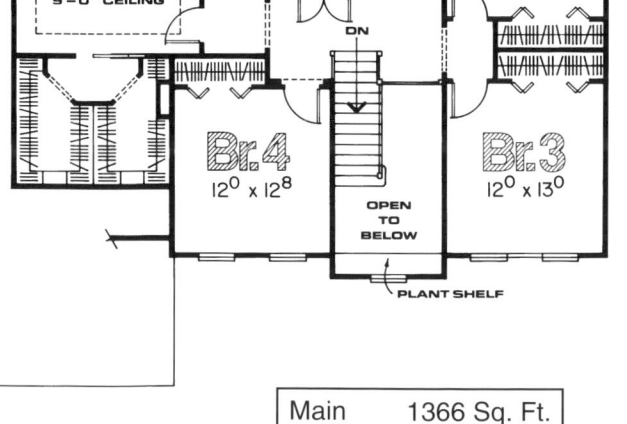

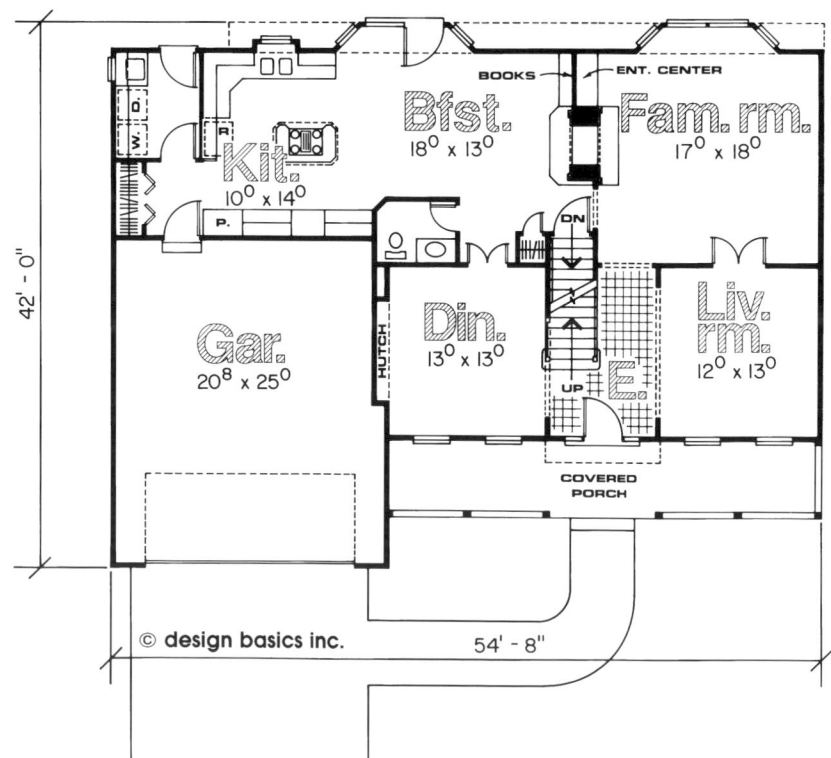

Main	1366 Sq. Ft.
Second	1278 Sq. Ft.
Total	2644 Sq. Ft.

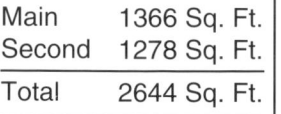

© design basics inc.

54' - 8"

42' - 0"

81

design basics inc.®
HOME PLAN DESIGN SERVICE

DUPLEX HOMES

LGS 4630 2x
PRICE CODE

► High quality, erasable, reproducible vellums
► Shipped via 2nd day air within the continental U.S.

Gold Seal HOME PLANS™

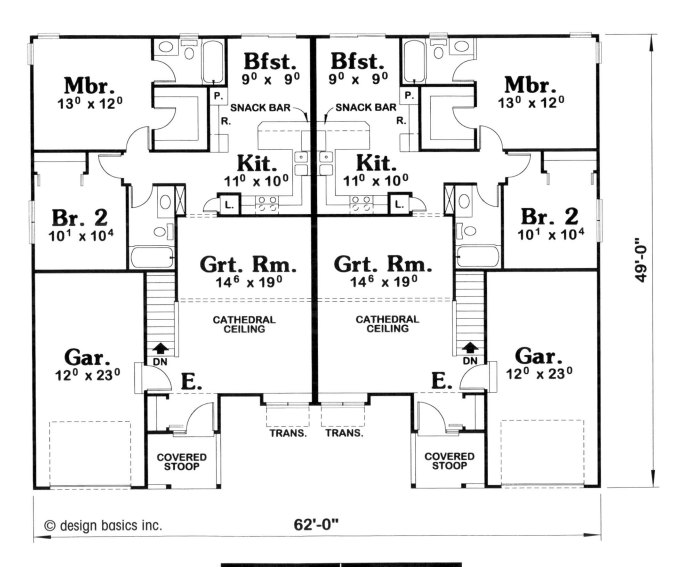

Mbr. 13⁰ x 12⁰

Bfst. 9⁰ x 9⁰

Bfst. 9⁰ x 9⁰

Mbr. 13⁰ x 12⁰

P.

P.

SNACK BAR

SNACK BAR

R.

R.

Kit. 11⁰ x 10⁰

Kit. 11⁰ x 10⁰

L.

L.

Br. 2 10¹ x 10⁴

Br. 2 10¹ x 10⁴

Grt. Rm. 14⁶ x 19⁰

Grt. Rm. 14⁶ x 19⁰

CATHEDRAL CEILING

CATHEDRAL CEILING

49'-0"

Gar. 12⁰ x 23⁰

DN

DN

Gar. 12⁰ x 23⁰

E.

E.

TRANS.

TRANS.

COVERED STOOP

COVERED STOOP

© design basics inc.

62'-0"

	LEFT SIDE	RIGHT SIDE
	Main 1079 sq. ft.	Main 1079 sq. ft.

ORDER DIRECT
7:00-6:00 Mon.-Fri. CST
800-947-PLAN

design basics inc. HOME PLAN DESIGN SERVICE

LGS 4626 2x

PRICE CODE

Gold Seal™
HOME PLANS

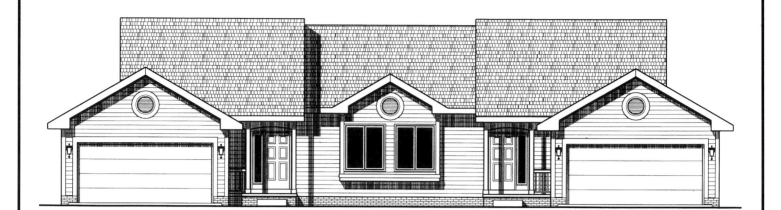

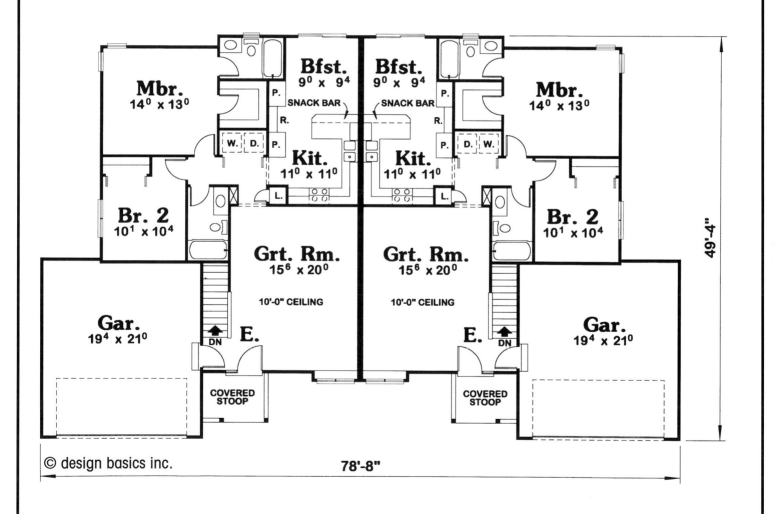

Mbr.
14⁰ x 13⁰

Bfst.
9⁰ x 9⁴

Bfst.
9⁰ x 9⁴

Mbr.
14⁰ x 13⁰

P.

SNACK BAR

SNACK BAR

P.

R.

R.

W. D.

P.

Kit.
11⁰ x 11⁰

Kit.
11⁰ x 11⁰

P.

D. W.

L.

L.

Br. 2
10¹ x 10⁴

Br. 2
10¹ x 10⁴

Grt. Rm.
15⁶ x 20⁰

Grt. Rm.
15⁶ x 20⁰

49'-4"

10'-0" CEILING

10'-0" CEILING

Gar.
19⁴ x 21⁰

Gar.
19⁴ x 21⁰

DN

E.

E.

DN

© design basics inc.

COVERED
STOOP

COVERED
STOOP

78'-8"

ORDER DIRECT

7:00-6:00 Mon.-Fri. CST

800-947-PLAN

	LEFT SIDE	RIGHT SIDE
Main	1140 sq. ft.	1140 sq. ft.

85

design basics inc.®
HOME PLAN DESIGN SERVICE

LGS 4614 2x

PRICE CODE

▸ High quality, erasable, reproducible vellums
▸ Shipped via 2nd day air within the continental U.S.

Gold Seal
HOME PLANS

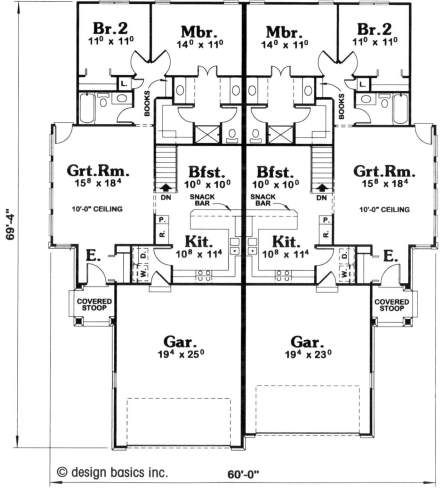

Br. 2
11⁰ x 11⁰

Mbr.
14⁰ x 11⁰

Mbr.
14⁰ x 11⁰

Br. 2
11⁰ x 11⁰

BOOKS

BOOKS

Grt. Rm.
15⁸ x 18⁴
10'-0" CEILING

Bfst.
10⁰ x 10⁰

Bfst.
10⁰ x 10⁰

Grt. Rm.
15⁸ x 18⁴
10'-0" CEILING

DN

DN

SNACK BAR

SNACK BAR

P. R.

P. R.

Kit.
10⁸ x 11⁴

Kit.
10⁸ x 11⁴

E.

W. D.

W. D.

E.

COVERED STOOP

COVERED STOOP

Gar.
19⁴ x 25⁰

Gar.
19⁴ x 23⁰

69'-4"

© design basics inc.

60'-0"

ORDER DIRECT
7:00-6:00 Mon.-Fri. CST
800-947-PLAN

	LEFT SIDE	RIGHT SIDE
Main	1218 sq. ft.	1218 sq. ft.

design basics inc.
HOME PLAN DESIGN SERVICE

LGS 4615 $2x$

PRICE CODE

▶ High quality, erasable, reproducible vellums
▶ Shipped via 2nd day air within the continental U.S.

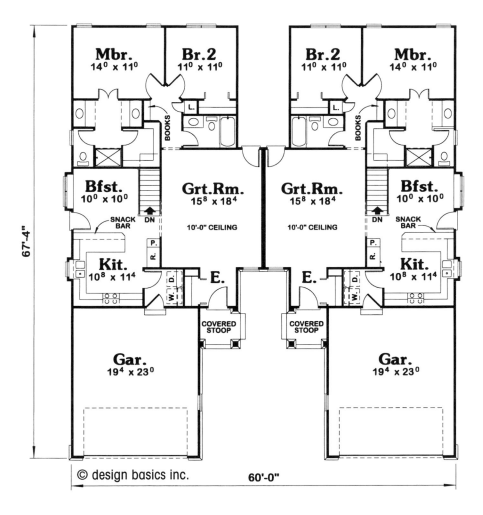

| Mbr. 14⁰ x 11⁰ | Br.2 11⁰ x 11⁰ | Br.2 11⁰ x 11⁰ | Mbr. 14⁰ x 11⁰ |

BOOKS

Bfst. 10⁰ x 10⁰

Grt.Rm. 15⁸ x 18⁴

10'-0" CEILING

Grt.Rm. 15⁸ x 18⁴

10'-0" CEILING

Bfst. 10⁰ x 10⁰

SNACK BAR

DN

SNACK BAR

DN

67'-4"

Kit. 10⁸ x 11⁴

E.

E.

Kit. 10⁸ x 11⁴

COVERED STOOP

COVERED STOOP

Gar. 19⁴ x 23⁰

Gar. 19⁴ x 23⁰

© design basics inc.

60'-0"

ORDER DIRECT

7:00-6:00 Mon.-Fri. CST

800-947-PLAN

	LEFT SIDE	RIGHT SIDE
Main	1218 sq. ft.	1218 sq. ft.

LGS 8174 PRICE CODE 2x

- ▸ High quality, erasable, reproducible vellums
- ▸ Shipped via 2nd day air within the continental U.S.

Gold Seal HOME PLANS™

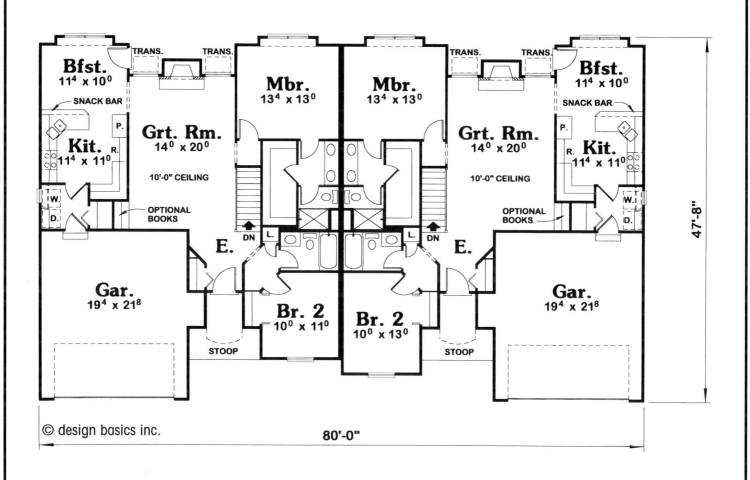

Bfst. 11⁴ x 10⁰

SNACK BAR

Kit. 11⁴ x 11⁰

TRANS. TRANS.

Grt. Rm. 14⁰ x 20⁰

10'-0" CEILING

OPTIONAL BOOKS

W. D.

Gar. 19⁴ x 21⁸

E. DN L.

STOOP

Mbr. 13⁴ x 13⁰

Br. 2 10⁰ x 11⁰

Mbr. 13⁴ x 13⁰

Br. 2 10⁰ x 13⁰

L. DN E.

STOOP

P. R.

Grt. Rm. 14⁰ x 20⁰

10'-0" CEILING

OPTIONAL BOOKS

TRANS. TRANS.

Bfst. 11⁴ x 10⁰

SNACK BAR

Kit. 11⁴ x 11⁰

W. D.

Gar. 19⁴ x 21⁸

47'-8"

© design basics inc.

80'-0"

ORDER DIRECT
7:00-6:00 Mon.-Fri. CST
800-947-PLAN

LEFT SIDE	RIGHT SIDE
Main 1212 sq. ft.	Main 1233 sq. ft.

88

design basics inc.
HOME PLAN DESIGN SERVICE

LGS 4623 2x

PRICE CODE

▶ High quality, erasable, reproducible vellums
▶ Shipped via 2nd day air within the continental U.S.

Gold Seal
HOME PLANS

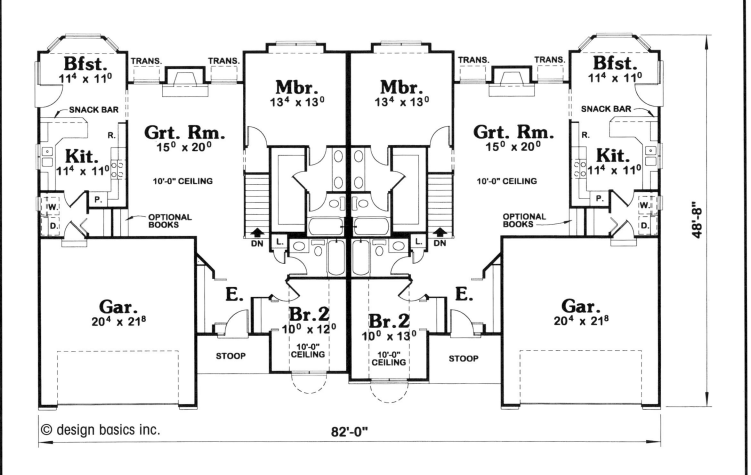

Bfst. 11⁴ x 11⁰

TRANS.   TRANS.

Mbr. 13⁴ x 13⁰

Mbr. 13⁴ x 13⁰

TRANS.   TRANS.

Bfst. 11⁴ x 11⁰

SNACK BAR

Kit. 11⁴ x 11⁰

R.

Grt. Rm. 15⁰ x 20⁰

10'-0" CEILING

Grt. Rm. 15⁰ x 20⁰

10'-0" CEILING

R.

SNACK BAR

Kit. 11⁴ x 11⁰

W.   P.
D.

OPTIONAL BOOKS

DN   L.

L.   DN

OPTIONAL BOOKS

P.   W.
D.

Gar. 20⁴ x 21⁸

E.

Br.2 10⁰ x 12⁰

10'-0" CEILING

Br.2 10⁰ x 13⁰

10'-0" CEILING

E.

Gar. 20⁴ x 21⁸

STOOP

STOOP

48'-8"

© design basics inc.

82'-0"

	LEFT SIDE	RIGHT SIDE
	Main 1242 sq. ft.	Main 1253 sq. ft.

design basics inc.
HOME PLAN DESIGN SERVICE

LGS 4620 PRICE CODE 2x

▸ High quality, erasable, reproducible vellums
▸ Shipped via 2nd day air within the continental U.S.

Gold Seal ™
HOME PLANS

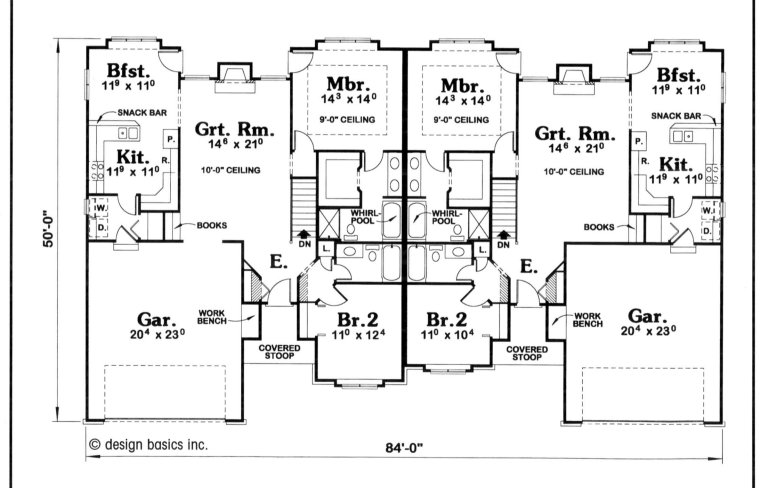

Bfst. 11⁹ x 11⁰

SNACK BAR

Kit. 11⁹ x 11⁰

Grt. Rm. 14⁶ x 21⁰

10'-0" CEILING

Mbr. 14³ x 14⁰

9'-0" CEILING

Mbr. 14³ x 14⁰

9'-0" CEILING

Grt. Rm. 14⁶ x 21⁰

10'-0" CEILING

SNACK BAR

Bfst. 11⁹ x 11⁰

Kit. 11⁹ x 11⁰

BOOKS

WHIRL-POOL

WHIRL-POOL

BOOKS

50'-0"

DN

L.

L.

DN

Gar. 20⁴ x 23⁰

WORK BENCH

E.

Br.2 11⁰ x 12⁴

Br.2 11⁰ x 10⁴

E.

WORK BENCH

Gar. 20⁴ x 23⁰

COVERED STOOP

COVERED STOOP

© design basics inc.

84'-0"

ORDER DIRECT
7:00-6:00 Mon.-Fri. CST
800-947-PLAN

	LEFT SIDE	RIGHT SIDE
	Main 1331 sq. ft.	Main 1308 sq. ft.

design basics inc.®
HOME PLAN DESIGN SERVICE

LGS 4625 PRICE CODE **2x**

▶ High quality, erasable, reproducible vellums
▶ Shipped via 2nd day air within the continental U.S.

Gold Seal ™
HOME PLANS

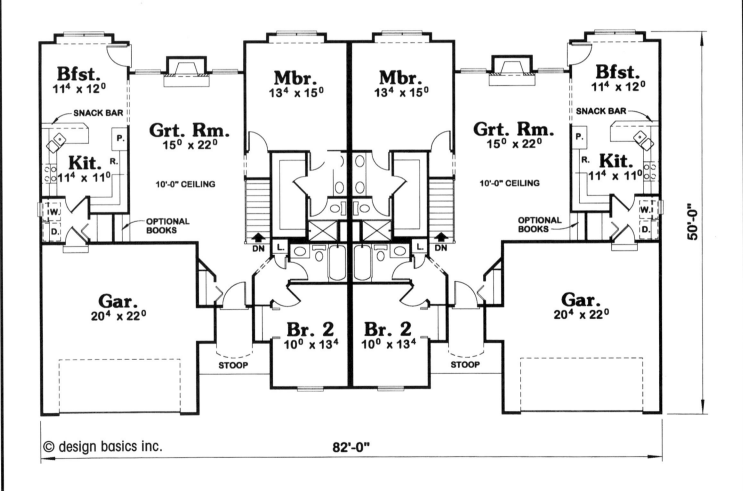

Bfst.
11⁴ x 12⁰

SNACK BAR

Grt. Rm.
15⁰ x 22⁰

Kit.
11⁴ x 11⁰

10'-0" CEILING

P.
R.

W
D

OPTIONAL BOOKS

Gar.
20⁴ x 22⁰

Mbr.
13⁴ x 15⁰

DN L

Br. 2
10⁰ x 13⁴

STOOP

Mbr.
13⁴ x 15⁰

L DN

Br. 2
10⁰ x 13⁴

STOOP

Grt. Rm.
15⁰ x 22⁰

10'-0" CEILING

OPTIONAL BOOKS

P.
R.

Bfst.
11⁴ x 12⁰

SNACK BAR

Kit.
11⁴ x 11⁰

W
D

Gar.
20⁴ x 22⁰

50'-0"

© design basics inc.

82'-0"

ORDER DIRECT
7:00-6:00 Mon.-Fri. CST
800-947-PLAN

	LEFT SIDE	RIGHT SIDE
Main	1344 sq. ft.	Main 1344 sq. ft.

design basics inc. ®
HOME PLAN DESIGN SERVICE

LGS 4629 2x

PRICE CODE

- ▶ High quality, erasable, reproducible vellums
- ▶ Shipped via 2nd day air within the continental U.S.

Gold Seal ™
HOME PLANS

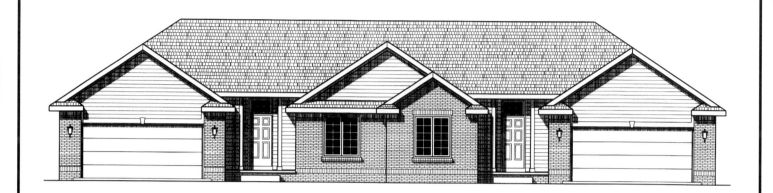

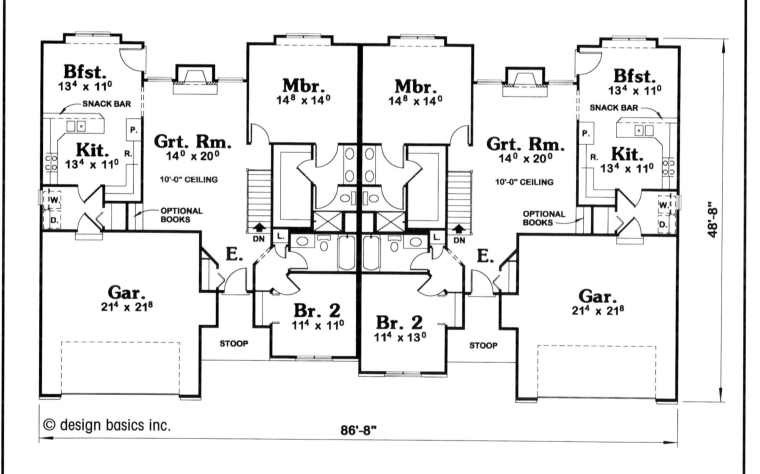

Bfst.
13⁴ x 11⁰

SNACK BAR

Kit.
13⁴ x 11⁰

P.

R.

Mbr.
14⁸ x 14⁰

Grt. Rm.
14⁰ x 20⁰

10'-0" CEILING

OPTIONAL
BOOKS

W.

D.

DN   L.

E.

Gar.
21⁴ x 21⁸

STOOP

Br. 2
11⁴ x 11⁰

Mbr.
14⁸ x 14⁰

Br. 2
11⁴ x 13⁰

STOOP

Grt. Rm.
14⁰ x 20⁰

10'-0" CEILING

OPTIONAL
BOOKS

L.   DN

E.

P.

R.

Bfst.
13⁴ x 11⁰

SNACK BAR

Kit.
13⁴ x 11⁰

W.

D.

Gar.
21⁴ x 21⁸

© design basics inc.

86'-8"

48'-8"

ORDER DIRECT
7:00-6:00 Mon.-Fri. CST
800-947-PLAN

	LEFT SIDE	RIGHT SIDE
	Main 1346 sq. ft.	Main 1370 sq. ft.

design basics inc.®
HOME PLAN DESIGN SERVICE

LGS 4618

PRICE CODE 2x

- High quality, erasable, reproducible vellums
- Shipped via 2nd day air within the continental U.S.

Gold Seal™
HOME PLANS

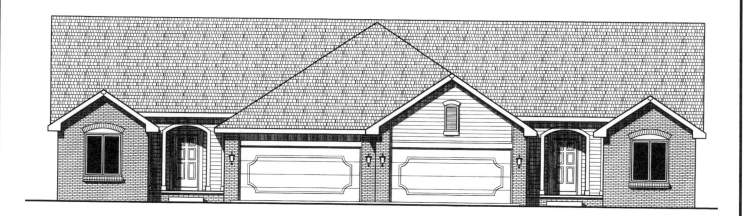

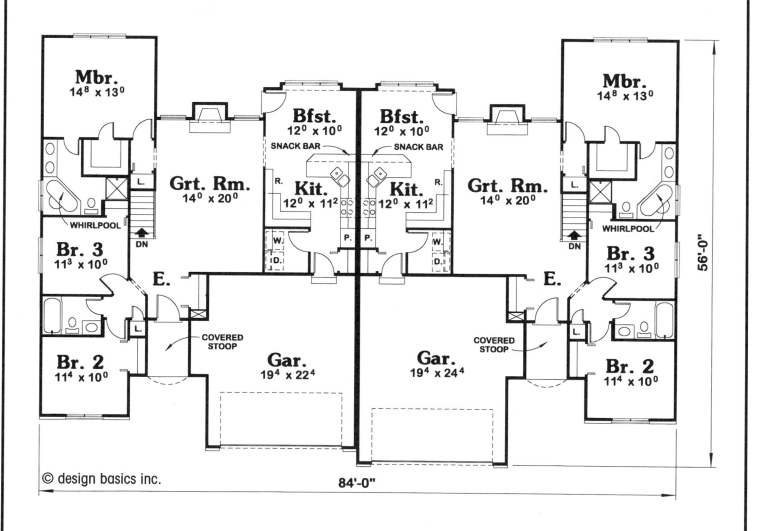

Mbr. 14⁸ x 13⁰

Grt. Rm. 14⁰ x 20⁰

Bfst. 12⁰ x 10⁰

SNACK BAR

Kit. 12⁰ x 11²

WHIRLPOOL

Br. 3 11³ x 10⁰

DN

E.

Br. 2 11⁴ x 10⁰

COVERED STOOP

Gar. 19⁴ x 22⁴

Bfst. 12⁰ x 10⁰

SNACK BAR

Kit. 12⁰ x 11²

Grt. Rm. 14⁰ x 20⁰

Mbr. 14⁸ x 13⁰

WHIRLPOOL

Br. 3 11³ x 10⁰

DN

E.

Br. 2 11⁴ x 10⁰

COVERED STOOP

Gar. 19⁴ x 24⁴

© design basics inc.

56'-0"

84'-0"

	LEFT SIDE	RIGHT SIDE
Main	1392 sq. ft.	Main 1392 sq. ft.

design basics inc.®
HOME PLAN DESIGN SERVICE

LGS 4631 PRICE CODE 2x

- ► High quality, erasable, reproducible vellums
- ► Shipped via 2nd day air within the continental U.S.

Gold Seal
HOME PLANS

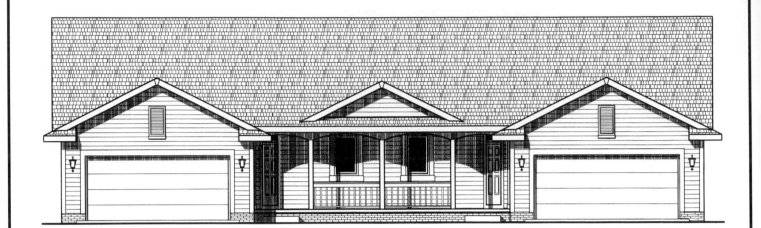

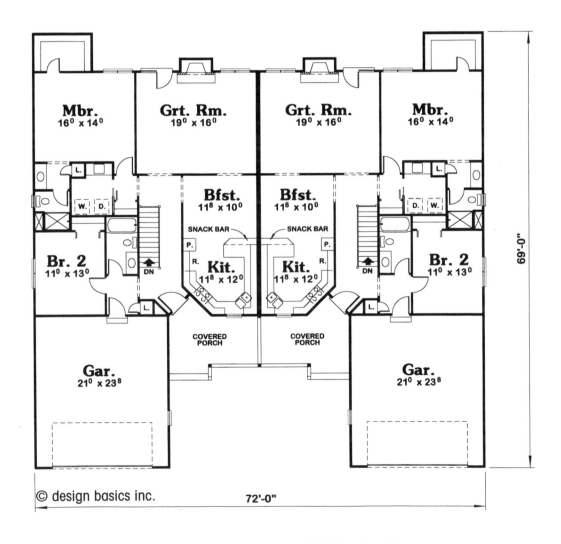

Mbr.
16⁰ x 14⁰

Grt. Rm.
19⁰ x 16⁰

Grt. Rm.
19⁰ x 16⁰

Mbr.
16⁰ x 14⁰

L.

W. D.

D. W.

L.

Bfst.
11⁸ x 10⁰

Bfst.
11⁸ x 10⁰

SNACK BAR

SNACK BAR

P.

P.

Br. 2
11⁰ x 13⁰

DN

R.

Kit.
11⁸ x 12⁰

Kit.
11⁸ x 12⁰

R.

DN

Br. 2
11⁰ x 13⁰

L.

L.

COVERED PORCH

COVERED PORCH

Gar.
21⁰ x 23⁸

Gar.
21⁰ x 23⁸

© design basics inc.

72'-0"

69'-0"

	LEFT SIDE	RIGHT SIDE
	Main 1455 sq. ft.	Main 1455 sq. ft.

ORDER DIRECT
7:00-6:00 Mon.-Fri. CST
800-947-PLAN

design basics inc.
HOME PLAN DESIGN SERVICE

94

LGS 4632 2x

PRICE CODE

▶ High quality, erasable, reproducible vellums
▶ Shipped via 2nd day air within the continental U.S.

Gold Seal ™
HOME PLANS

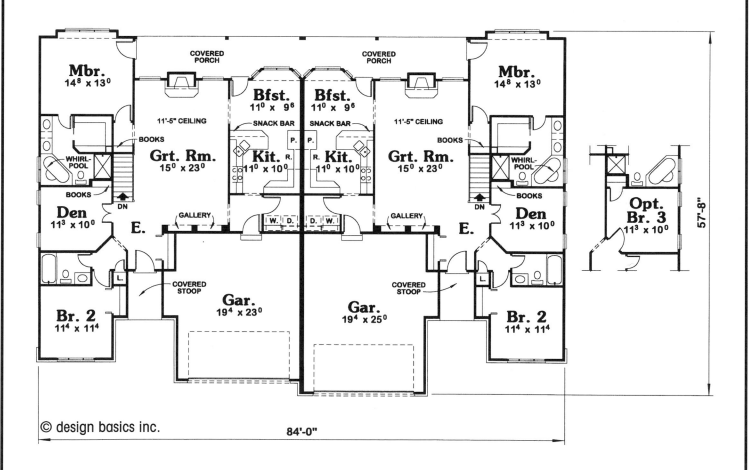

Mbr. 14⁸ x 13⁰

COVERED PORCH

COVERED PORCH

Mbr. 14⁸ x 13⁰

11'-5" CEILING

Bfst. 11⁰ x 9⁶

Bfst. 11⁰ x 9⁶

11'-5" CEILING

BOOKS

SNACK BAR

SNACK BAR

BOOKS

WHIRL-POOL

Grt. Rm. 15⁰ x 23⁰

P.

R.

Kit. 11⁰ x 10⁰

Kit. 11⁰ x 10⁰

R.

P.

Grt. Rm. 15⁰ x 23⁰

WHIRL-POOL

BOOKS

BOOKS

DN

DN

Den 11³ x 10⁰

Opt. Br. 3 11³ x 10⁰

57'-8"

E.

GALLERY

W. D.   D. W.

GALLERY

E.

Den 11³ x 10⁰

L.

COVERED STOOP

COVERED STOOP

L.

Br. 2 11⁴ x 11⁴

Gar. 19⁴ x 23⁰

Gar. 19⁴ x 25⁰

Br. 2 11⁴ x 11⁴

© design basics inc.

84'-0"

ORDER DIRECT
7:00-6:00 Mon.-Fri. CST
800-947-PLAN

	LEFT SIDE	RIGHT SIDE
	Main 1478 sq. ft.	Main 1478 sq. ft.

design basics inc. ®
HOME PLAN DESIGN SERVICE

95

LGS 4619 PRICE CODE 2x

▶ High quality, erasable, reproducible vellums
▶ Shipped via 2nd day air within the continental U.S.

Gold Seal
HOME PLANS

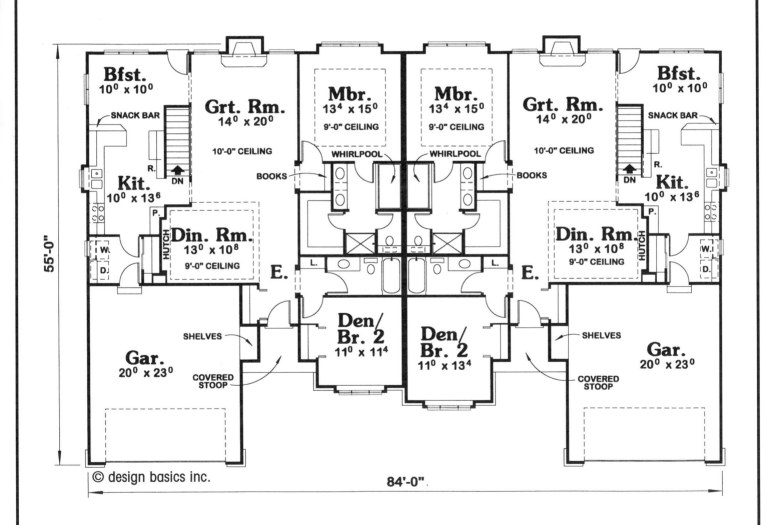

Bfst.
10⁰ x 10⁰

SNACK BAR

Grt. Rm.
14⁰ x 20⁰

10'-0" CEILING

Mbr.
13⁴ x 15⁰
9'-0" CEILING

Mbr.
13⁴ x 15⁰
9'-0" CEILING

Grt. Rm.
14⁰ x 20⁰

10'-0" CEILING

Bfst.
10⁰ x 10⁰

SNACK BAR

R.   DN

WHIRLPOOL   WHIRLPOOL

DN   R.

Kit.
10⁰ x 13⁶

BOOKS   BOOKS

Kit.
10⁰ x 13⁶

P.   HUTCH

Din. Rm.
13⁰ x 10⁸
9'-0" CEILING

L.   L.

Din. Rm.
13⁰ x 10⁸
9'-0" CEILING

HUTCH   P.

W.   D.

E.   E.

W.   D.

55'-0"

SHELVES

Gar.
20⁰ x 23⁰

COVERED
STOOP

**Den/
Br. 2**
11⁰ x 11⁴

**Den/
Br. 2**
11⁰ x 13⁴

COVERED
STOOP

SHELVES

Gar.
20⁰ x 23⁰

© design basics inc.

84'-0".

ORDER DIRECT
7:00-6:00 Mon.-Fri. CST
800-947-PLAN

	LEFT SIDE	RIGHT SIDE
	Main 1516 sq. ft.	Main 1539 sq. ft.

design basics inc.®
HOME PLAN DESIGN SERVICE

LGS 4616 PRICE CODE 2x

▶ High quality, erasable, reproducible vellums
▶ Shipped via 2nd day air within the continental U.S.

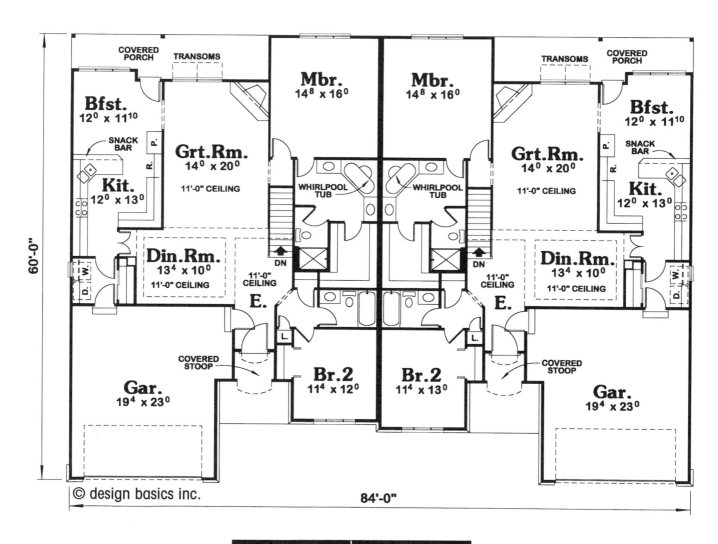

COVERED PORCH   TRANSOMS

Bfst.
12⁰ x 11¹⁰

Mbr.
14⁸ x 16⁰

Mbr.
14⁸ x 16⁰

TRANSOMS   COVERED PORCH

Bfst.
12⁰ x 11¹⁰

SNACK BAR

Grt.Rm.
14⁰ x 20⁰
11'-0" CEILING

WHIRLPOOL TUB

WHIRLPOOL TUB

Grt.Rm.
14⁰ x 20⁰
11'-0" CEILING

SNACK BAR

Kit.
12⁰ x 13⁰

Kit.
12⁰ x 13⁰

Din.Rm.
13⁴ x 10⁰
11'-0" CEILING

DN

DN

Din.Rm.
13⁴ x 10⁰
11'-0" CEILING

60'-0"

E.

11'-0" CEILING

11'-0" CEILING

E.

COVERED STOOP

COVERED STOOP

Gar.
19⁴ x 23⁰

Br.2
11⁴ x 12⁰

Br.2
11⁴ x 13⁰

Gar.
19⁴ x 23⁰

© design basics inc.

84'-0"

	LEFT SIDE	RIGHT SIDE
Main	1633 sq. ft.	Main 1645 sq. ft.

ORDER DIRECT
7:00-6:00 Mon.-Fri. CST
800-947-PLAN

▶ High quality, erasable, reproducible vellums
▶ Shipped via 2nd day air within the continental U.S.

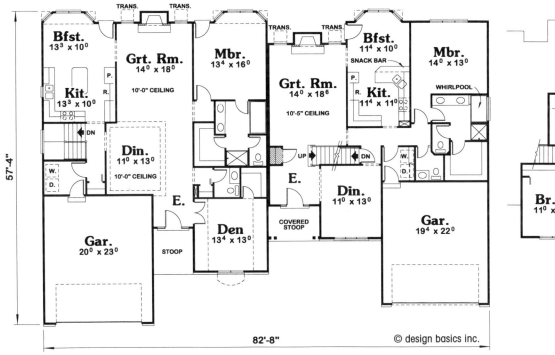

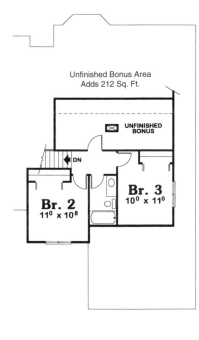

© design basics inc.

LEFT SIDE	RIGHT SIDE	
	Main	1324 sq. ft.
Main 1621 sq. ft.	Second	391 sq. ft.
	Total	1715 sq. ft.

LGS 4633 PRICE CODE 2x

▶ High quality, erasable, reproducible vellums
▶ Shipped via 2nd day air within the continental U.S.

Unfinished Bonus Area
Adds 212 Sq. Ft.

UNFINISHED BONUS

Br. 2
10⁰ x 11⁰

DN

Br. 3
11⁰ x 10⁸

Br. 3
11⁰ x 10⁸

DN

UNFINISHED BONUS

Br. 2
10⁰ x 11⁰

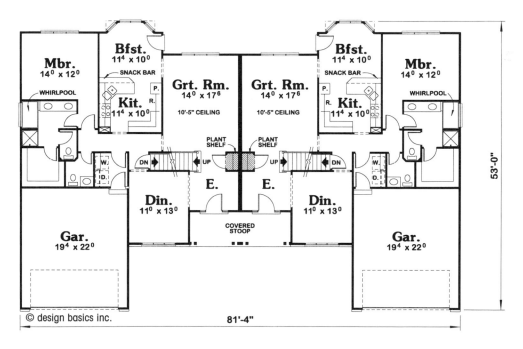

Mbr.
14⁰ x 12⁰

WHIRLPOOL

Bfst.
11⁴ x 10⁰

SNACK BAR

Kit.
11⁴ x 10⁰

Grt. Rm.
14⁰ x 17⁶
10'-5" CEILING

Grt. Rm.
14⁰ x 17⁶
10'-5" CEILING

Bfst.
11⁴ x 10⁰

SNACK BAR

Kit.
11⁴ x 10⁰

Mbr.
14⁰ x 12⁰

WHIRLPOOL

PLANT SHELF

PLANT SHELF

DN   UP

UP   DN

W.
I.D.

E.

E.

W.
I.D.

Din.
11⁰ x 13⁰

Din.
11⁰ x 13⁰

53'-0"

Gar.
19⁴ x 22⁰

COVERED STOOP

Gar.
19⁴ x 22⁰

© design basics inc.

81'-4"

ORDER DIRECT
7:00-6:00 Mon.-Fri. CST

800-947-PLAN

	LEFT SIDE	RIGHT SIDE
Main	1284 sq. ft.	Main 1284 sq. ft.
Second	391 sq. ft.	Second 391 sq. ft.
Total	1675 sq. ft.	Total 1675 sq. ft.

LGS 4627 PRICE CODE 2x

Gold Seal ™
HOME PLANS

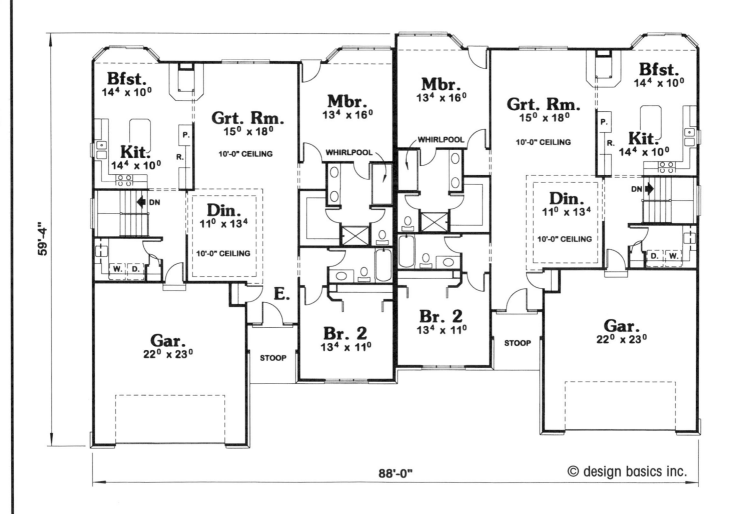

Bfst. 14⁴ x 10⁰

Kit. 14⁴ x 10⁰

Grt. Rm. 15⁰ x 18⁰
10'-0" CEILING

P. R.

Din. 11⁰ x 13⁴
10'-0" CEILING

W. D.

Mbr. 13⁴ x 16⁰

WHIRLPOOL

Mbr. 13⁴ x 16⁰

WHIRLPOOL

Grt. Rm. 15⁰ x 18⁰
10'-0" CEILING

P. R.

Bfst. 14⁴ x 10⁰

Kit. 14⁴ x 10⁰

DN

Din. 11⁰ x 13⁴
10'-0" CEILING

D. W.

59'-4"

Gar. 22⁰ x 23⁰

STOOP

E.

Br. 2 13⁴ x 11⁰

Br. 2 13⁴ x 11⁰

STOOP

Gar. 22⁰ x 23⁰

88'-0"

© design basics inc.

	LEFT SIDE	RIGHT SIDE
	Main 1685 sq. ft.	Main 1685 sq. ft.

design basics inc. ®
HOME PLAN DESIGN SERVICE

LGS 4622 2x

PRICE CODE

Gold Seal™
HOME PLANS

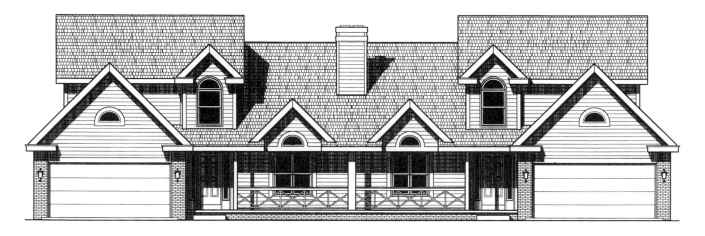

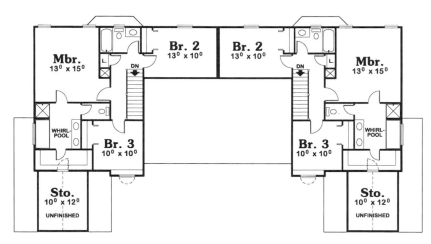

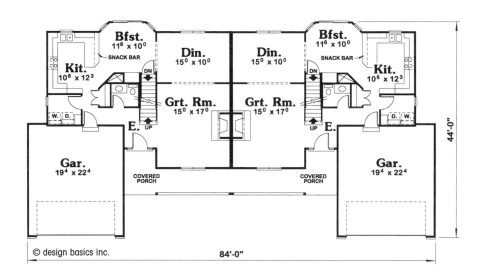

© design basics inc.   84'-0"

	LEFT SIDE	RIGHT SIDE
Main	918 sq. ft.	Main 918 sq. ft.
Second	802 sq. ft.	Second 802 sq. ft.
Total	1720 sq. ft.	Total 1720 sq. ft.

design basics inc.®
HOME PLAN DESIGN SERVICE

LGS 4617 2x

PRICE CODE

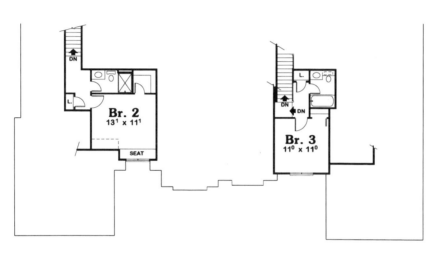

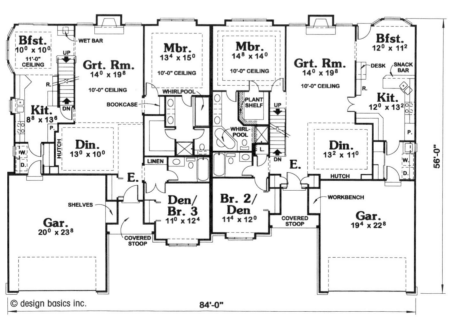

© design basics inc.

84'-0"

	LEFT SIDE	RIGHT SIDE
Main	1486 sq. ft.	1517 sq. ft.
Second	286 sq. ft.	234 sq. ft.
Total	1772 sq. ft.	1751 sq. ft.

HOME PLAN DESIGN SERVICE

▶ High quality, erasable, reproducible vellums
▶ Shipped via 2nd day air within the continental U.S.

Gold Seal™
HOME PLANS

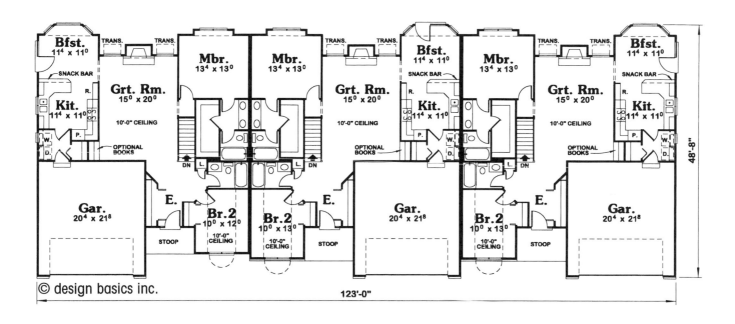

© design basics inc.

123'-0"

48'-8"

	LEFT SIDE	MIDDLE	RIGHT SIDE
	Main 1242 sq. ft.	Main 1253 sq. ft.	Main 1253 sq. ft.

ORDER DIRECT
7:00-6:00 Mon.-Fri. CST
800-947-PLAN

design basics inc.®
HOME PLAN DESIGN SERVICE

► High quality, erasable, reproducible vellums
► Shipped via 2nd day air within the continental U.S.

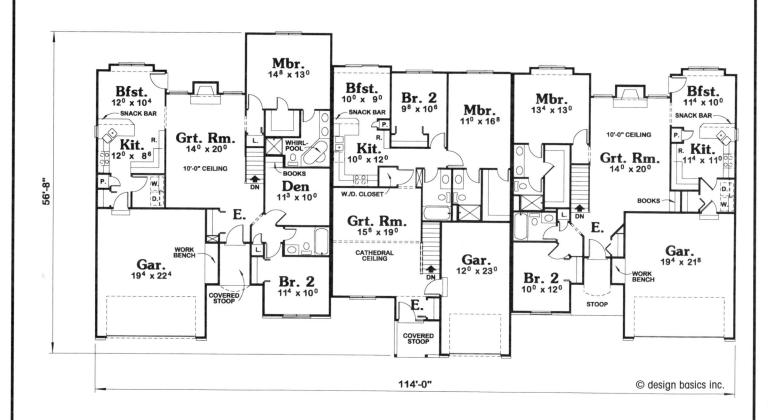

114'-0"

56'-8"

© design basics inc.

	LEFT SIDE	MIDDLE	RIGHT SIDE
	Main 1393 sq. ft.	Main 1160 sq. ft.	Main 1223 sq. ft.

ORDER DIRECT
7:00-6:00 Mon.-Fri. CST
800-947-PLAN

LGS 4011

▶ High quality, erasable, reproducible vellums
▶ Shipped via 2nd day air within the continental U.S.

Gold Seal
HOME PLANS™

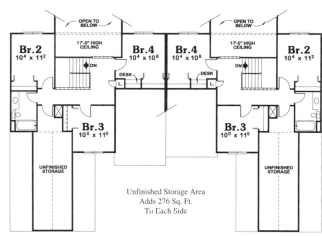

Br. 2
10⁴ x 11²

OPEN TO BELOW

17'-0" HIGH CEILING

Br. 4
10⁴ x 10⁶

DN

DESK

Br. 4
10⁴ x 10⁶

OPEN TO BELOW

17'-0" HIGH CEILING

DN

DESK

Br. 2
10⁴ x 11²

Br. 3
10⁰ x 11⁰

Br. 3
10⁰ x 11⁰

UNFINISHED STORAGE

UNFINISHED STORAGE

Unfinished Storage Area
Adds 276 Sq. Ft.
To Each Side

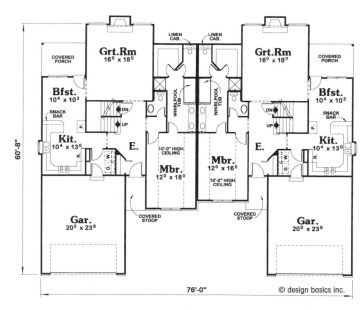

COVERED PORCH

Grt. Rm
16⁰ x 18⁰

LINEN CAB.

LINEN CAB.

Grt. Rm
16⁰ x 18⁰

COVERED PORCH

Bfst.
10⁴ x 10³

SNACK BAR

Kit.
10⁴ x 13⁰

DN

UP

WHIRLPOOL TUB

WHIRLPOOL TUB

DN

UP

Bfst.
10⁴ x 10³

SNACK BAR

Kit.
10⁴ x 13⁰

E.

10'-0" HIGH CEILING

Mbr.
12⁰ x 18⁰

Mbr.
12⁰ x 16⁰

10'-0" HIGH CEILING

E.

Gar.
20⁰ x 23⁸

COVERED STOOP

COVERED STOOP

Gar.
20⁰ x 23⁸

60'-8"

76'-0"

© design basics inc.

ORDER DIRECT
7:00-6:00 Mon.-Fri. CST
800-947-PLAN

	LEFT SIDE	RIGHT SIDE
Main	1308 sq. ft.	Main 1284 sq. ft.
Second	645 sq. ft.	Second 645 sq. ft.
Total	1953 sq. ft.	Total 1929 sq. ft.

design basics inc.®
HOME PLAN DESIGN SERVICE

LGS 4628

▶ High quality, erasable, reproducible vellums
▶ Shipped via 2nd day air within the continental U.S.

Gold Seal™
HOME PLANS

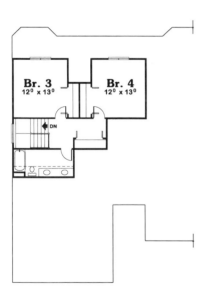

Br. 3
12⁰ x 13⁰

Br. 4
12⁰ x 13⁰

DN

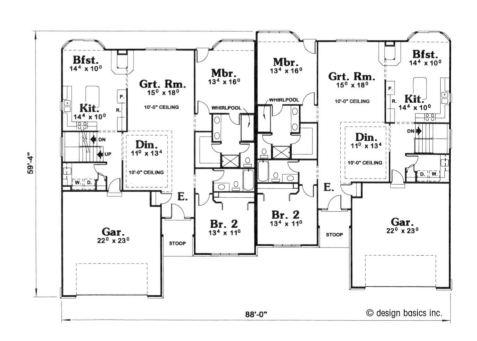

Bfst.
14⁴ x 10⁰

Kit.
14⁴ x 10⁰

Grt. Rm.
15⁰ x 18⁰
10'-0" CEILING

P.
R.

DN

UP

Din.
11⁰ x 13⁴
10'-0" CEILING

W. D.

Mbr.
13⁴ x 16⁰

WHIRLPOOL

Mbr.
13⁴ x 16⁰

WHIRLPOOL

Grt. Rm.
15⁰ x 18⁰
10'-0" CEILING

P.
R.

DN

Bfst.
14⁴ x 10⁰

Kit.
14⁴ x 10⁰

Din.
11⁰ x 13⁴
10'-0" CEILING

D. W.

Gar.
22⁰ x 23⁰

STOOP

E.

Br. 2
13⁴ x 11⁰

Br. 2
13⁴ x 11⁰

STOOP

E.

Gar.
22⁰ x 23⁰

59'-4"

88'-0"

© design basics inc.

ORDER DIRECT
7:00-6:00 Mon.-Fri. CST
800-947-PLAN

LEFT SIDE	RIGHT SIDE
Main 1685 sq. ft.	
Second 576 sq. ft.	Main 1685 sq. ft.
Total 2261 sq. ft.	

design basics inc.®
HOME PLAN DESIGN SERVICE

LGS 4012 2x

PRICE CODE

Gold Seal
HOME PLANS

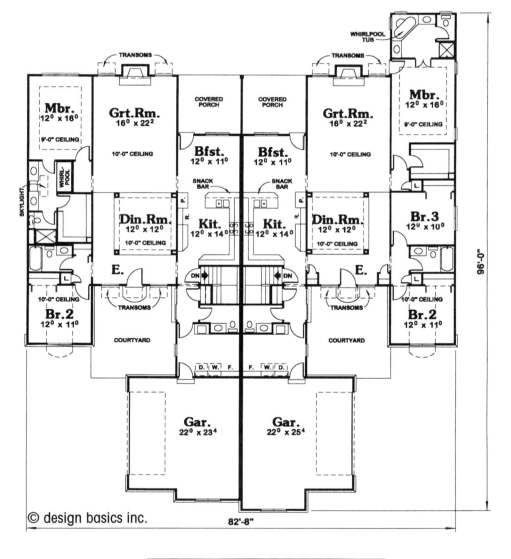

WHIRLPOOL TUB

TRANSOMS

Mbr.
12⁰ x 16⁰
9'-0" CEILING

Grt.Rm.
16⁰ x 22²
10'-0" CEILING

COVERED PORCH

COVERED PORCH

Grt.Rm.
16⁰ x 22²
10'-0" CEILING

Mbr.
12⁰ x 16⁰
9'-0" CEILING

WHIRL-POOL

Bfst.
12⁰ x 11⁰

Bfst.
12⁰ x 11⁰

SKYLIGHT

SNACK BAR

SNACK BAR

Din.Rm.
12⁰ x 12⁰
10'-0" CEILING

Kit.
12⁰ x 14⁰

Kit.
12⁰ x 14⁰

Din.Rm.
12⁰ x 12⁰
10'-0" CEILING

Br.3
12⁰ x 10⁰

E.

DN

DN

E.

96'-0"

10'-0" CEILING

Br.2
12⁰ x 11⁰

TRANSOMS

TRANSOMS

10'-0" CEILING

Br.2
12⁰ x 11⁰

COURTYARD

COURTYARD

D. W. F.

F. W. D.

Gar.
22⁰ x 23⁴

Gar.
22⁰ x 25⁴

© design basics inc.

82'-8"

ORDER DIRECT
7:00-6:00 Mon.-Fri. CST
800-947-PLAN

	LEFT SIDE	RIGHT SIDE
Main	1908 sq. ft.	Main 2060 sq. ft.

design basics inc.
HOME PLAN DESIGN SERVICE

LGS 4621 4x

PRICE CODE

- ▶ High quality, erasable, reproducible vellums
- ▶ Shipped via 2nd day air within the continental U.S.

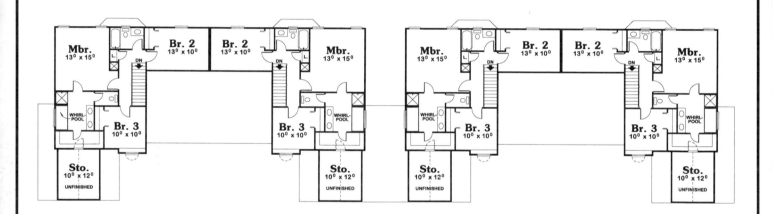

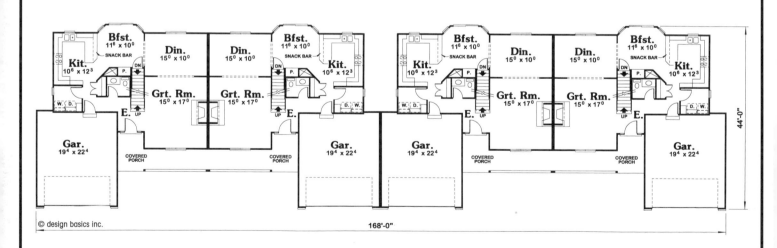

© design basics inc.

168'-0"

44'-0"

ORDER DIRECT
7:00-6:00 Mon.-Fri. CST
800-947-PLAN

HOME PLAN DESIGN SERVICE

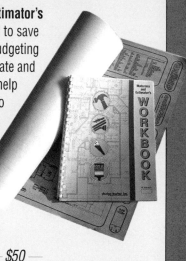

Quality Plans ~ Dependable Designs

Design Basics home plans come to you on high-quality, erasable, reproducible vellums and include the following:

1. COVER PAGE. Each Design Basics home plan features the rendered elevation and floor plans and informative reference sections including: general notes and design criteria* ; abbreviations; and symbols for your Design Basics plan.

2. ELEVATIONS. Fully detailed showing materials used, and drafted at $1/4$" scale for the front and $1/8$" scale for the rear and sides. An aerial view of the roof is provided showing all hips, valleys and ridges. For a more thorough understanding, a Roof Construction Package (see below) is available showing roof framing and dimensional layouts. Additionally, fascia and railing sections are provided when necessary.

3. FOUNDATIONS. Drafted at $1/4$" scale. Block foundations and basements are standard. We also show the suggested HVAC layout, structural information* , steel beam and pole locations and the direction and spacing of the floor system above.

4. MAIN LEVEL FLOOR PLAN. $1/4$" scale. Fully dimensioned from stud to stud for ease of framing. 2"x4" walls are standard. The detailed drawings include such things as ceiling treatments, structural header locations , flooring materials, framing layout, supply air locations and kitchen layout.

5. SECOND LEVEL FLOOR PLAN. $1/4$" scale. Dimensioned from stud to stud and drafted to the same degree of detail as the main level floor plan* .

6. INTERIOR ELEVATIONS. Useful for the cabinet and bidding process, this page shows all kitchen and bathroom cabinets as well as any other cabinet elevations. Also shown is the elevation of the fireplace face, designed to complement the overall theme of the house.

7. ELECTRICAL AND SECTIONS. Illustrated on a separate page for clarity, the electrical plan shows suggested electrical layout for the foundation, main and second-level floor plans. Typical wall, cantilever, stair, brick and fireplace sections are provided to further explain construction of these areas.

CODES AND CONDITIONS

Our plans are drafted to meet average codes and conditions in the state of Nebraska, at the time they are designed. Because codes and requirements can change and may vary from jurisdiction to jurisdiction, Design Basics Inc. cannot warrant compliance with any specific code or regulation. All Design Basics plans can be adapted to your local building codes and requirements. It is the responsibility of the purchaser and/or builder of each plan to see that the structure is built in strict compliance with all governing municipal codes (city, county, state and federal).

ERASABLE VELLUMS

Before making changes to your plan, PLEASE NOTE the following.
- *To erase, you must use an electric eraser with a white #73 refill (we recommend a Eberhard Faber refill #75214.)*
- *Use a 2H graphite lead to re-draft.*

If you have any further questions, call one of our Customer Support Specialists at (800) 947-7526.

Don't Underestimate our Roofs!

Roof Construction Package
- NOT AVAILABLE -
FOR DUPLEX PLANS

- *Prepare accurate bids.*
- *Eliminate costly mistakes and waste.*
- *Save time and money during construction.*

Our Roof Construction Package is a complete roof framing and dimensional layout, including:

1) Aerial views of the roof showing hips, valleys, ridges, rafters and roof supports.
2) A dimensional plan showing lengths, runs, ridge heights and wall plate heights.

$100 at time of plan purchase. *$150 after plan purchase.
*Please have Construction License Number Available

CUSTOMIZED PLAN CHANGES

PRICE SCHEDULE

ALL PLANS *Customizable*

2 X 6 EXTERIOR WALLS .... $150 .....
FROM STANDARD 2 X 4 TO 2 X 6 EXTERIOR WALLS

EACH GARAGE ALTERATION .... $275 .....
- FRONT-ENTRY TO SIDE LOAD (OR VICE VERSA)
- 2-CAR TO 3-CAR (OR VICE VERSA)
- 2-CAR FRONT-ENTRY TO 3-CAR SIDE -LOAD (OR VICE VERSA)
- 3-CAR FRONT-ENTRY TO 2-CAR SIDE -LOAD (OR VICE VERSA)

WALK-OUT BASEMENT .... $175 .....

CRAWL SPACE FOUNDATION .... $225 .....

SLAB FOUNDATION .... $225 .....

STRETCH CHANGES .... $5 per lineal foot of cut

ADDITIONAL BRICK TO SIDES & REAR .... $325 .....

ADDITIONAL BRICK TO FRONT,
   SIDES AND REAR .... $425 .....

ALTERNATE PRELIMINARY ELEVATION .... $150 .....

9-FOOT MAIN LEVEL WALLS.............................. starting at $150

SPECIFY WINDOW BRAND .... $95 .....

POURED CONCRETE FOUNDATION .... $25 .....
   ONLY WITH OTHER CHANGES

ADDING ONE COURSE (8") TO THE FOUNDATION HEIGHT
   ONLY WITH OTHER CHANGES .... $25 .....

* PRICES HIGHER FOR DUPLEX PLANS, CALL (800) 947-7526 FOR DETAILS.

NOTE ....
- All plan changes come to you on erasable, reproducible vellums.
- An unchanged set of original vellums is available for only $50 along with your plan changes.
- Gold Seal™ changes are not made to the artist's renderings, electrical, sections or cabinets.
- Prices are subject to change.

As a part of our commitment to help you achieve the "perfect" home, we offer an extensive variety of plan changes for any Design Basics plan. For those whose decision to purchase a home plan is contingent upon the feasibility of a plan change, our Customer Support Specialists will, in most cases, be able to provide a FREE price quote for the changes.

call us toll-free at

(800) 947-7526

to order plan changes listed here, or if you have questions regarding plan changes not listed.

ORDERING INFORMATION – ATTENTION DEPT. 9L

Name _____

Address _____
(For UPS Delivery – Packages cannot be shipped to a P.O. Box.)

Above Address ☐ business address ☐ residence address

☐ Visa *VISA* ☐ AMEX

☐ MasterCard *MasterCard* ☐ Discover *DISCOVER NOVUS*

☐ Check enclosed

Credit Card:

All COD's must be paid by Certified Check, Cashier's Check or Money Order.
(Additional $5.00 charge on COD orders)

Company _____

Title _____

City _____ State _____ Zip _____

Phone ( ) _____ FAX ( ) _____

☐☐ / ☐☐
Expiration Date

Signature _____

Follow this example for ordering PLANS:

PLAN NUMBER	PLAN NAME	AMOUNT
LGS - 2779	Leawood	$595
Additional set of prints w/plan purchase	ea. $10.00	
	SUBTOTAL	

Follow this example for ordering PRODUCTS and BOOKS:

PLAN NUMBER	DESCRIPTION	QTY.	AMOUNT
LGS - 2779	Materials and Estimator's Workbook	1	$50

BOOK NAME / DESCRIPTION	QTY.	AMOUNT

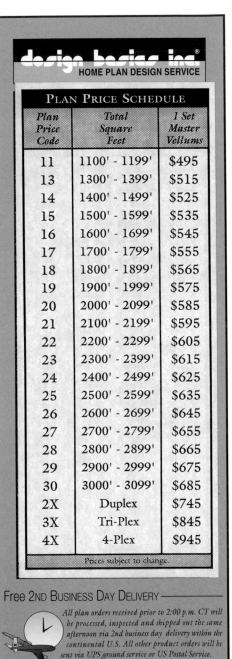

design basics inc.®
HOME PLAN DESIGN SERVICE

PLAN PRICE SCHEDULE

Plan Price Code	Total Square Feet	1 Set Master Vellums
11	1100' - 1199'	$495
13	1300' - 1399'	$515
14	1400' - 1499'	$525
15	1500' - 1599'	$535
16	1600' - 1699'	$545
17	1700' - 1799'	$555
18	1800' - 1899'	$565
19	1900' - 1999'	$575
20	2000' - 2099'	$585
21	2100' - 2199'	$595
22	2200' - 2299'	$605
23	2300' - 2399'	$615
24	2400' - 2499'	$625
25	2500' - 2599'	$635
26	2600' - 2699'	$645
27	2700' - 2799'	$655
28	2800' - 2899'	$665
29	2900' - 2999'	$675
30	3000' - 3099'	$685
2X	Duplex	$745
3X	Tri-Plex	$845
4X	4-Plex	$945

Prices subject to change.

SHIPPING & HANDLING
(CONTINENTAL US)

Home plans
2nd Business Day . . . . N/C
Next Business Day $15.00

Books & Products
UPS Ground (4-5 business days) . . . . $ 4.95
2nd Business Day $10.00
Next Business Day $20.00
Any Single Plan Books . . . . $ 2.95
Any Combination of Plan Books . . . . $ 4.95
SAME DAY SHIPPING IF ORDERED BY 2:00 P.M. CT.

SUBTOTAL OF PLANS, PRODUCTS AND BOOKS

NE Res. Add 6.5% Sales Tax

Shipping & Handling (see chart at left)

No refunds or exchanges, please.
All orders payable in U.S. funds only.

TOTAL

Free 2ND BUSINESS DAY DELIVERY

All plan orders received prior to 2:00 p.m. CT will be processed, inspected and shipped out the same afternoon via 2nd business day delivery within the continental U.S. All other product orders will be sent via UPS ground service or US Postal Service.

All Design Basics home plans come with a basement foundation. Alternate foundations available for additional charges. Home plans do not carry an architect's/engineer's stamp. You may need to obtain an architect's/engineer's stamp to comply with your local building codes.

FOR FASTEST SERVICE CALL (800) 947-7526 OR FAX (402) 331-5507
Monday - Friday, 7:00 a.m. to 6:00 p.m. C.T.
Design Basics Inc. • 11112 John Galt Boulevard • Omaha, Nebraska 68137-2384

STANDARDS OF EXCELLENCE — *Each complete Gold Seal™ Home Plan design comes to you on high quality, erasable, reproducible vellum.*